mayylu!

Discovering Lebanon's Hidden Culinary Heritage

mayylu!

Discovering Lebanon's Hidden Culinary Heritage

A FOODBOOK BY
HANA EL-HIBRI

I dedicate this book to my mom, Hindo, who instilled in me the value of hospitality and the pleasure of cooking for family and friends.

Copyright text © Hana El-Hibri 2019
Copyright all images © CC 2019, apart from: Maya Alameddine: p34 top right; Belal El-Hibri: p13; Walid Rashid: p37 top left
Cover images: Jana Traboulsi: front cover illustration; Kristine Khouri: back flap author photo

Editorial: Michael Karam, Alex Newby, Melissa Scott
Colour correction: Marc Merhej

Published by Gilgamesh Publishing in 2019
Email: info@gilgamesh-publishing.co.uk
www.gilgamesh-publishing.co.uk
ISBN 978-190853-197-1

All rights are reserved. No part of this publication may be reproduced, stored in a retrieval system or transmitted in any form or by any means, electronic, mechanical, photographic or otherwise, without prior permission of the copyright holder.
CIP Data: A catalogue for this book is available from the British Library

CONTENTS

Foreword	9
Introduction	10
On the Wild Side	12

THE NORTH — 14

ANDQET, **Hana Shaar** — 18
Jermesh	20
Kibbeh Bil Addass Wal Shumar (Lentil and Fennel Kebbeh)	22
Krass Qameh	24

ASSIA, **Sana Jabbour** — 26
Mtabbsseh (Zinkol with Onions)	30
Mattmoura (Slow Cooked Clay Baked Chicken)	32

AQOURA, **Guitta & Philippe Germanos** — 34
Batata Bi Joz (Walnut Mashed Potaoes)	38
Slatet Korra Wa Jarjeer (Water Parsnip and Rocket Salad)	40
Maacroon Bi Labneh Wa Qawarma (Gnocchis in Yoghurt and Qawarma)	42
Tbaybisseh	44

BQAA SEFRINE, **Imm Majed** — 46
Fatayer Bil Siliq Wa Joz (Swiss Chard and Walnut Turnovers)	48
Siliq Bil Loubiyeh (Swiss Chard with Green Beans)	50
Koussa Mtabbal (Sautéed Courgettes)	52
Shish Barak Ma Moudardara (Goat Yoghurt Shish Barak with Lentil Pilaf)	54

BAINO, **Samia & Marwan Naufal** — 58
Batinjan Mikli (Low Oil Fried Eggplant)	60
Kibbeh Bawabneh	62
Lahm Bi Khal (Meat in Vinegar Sauce)	64

DOUMA, **Guitta Yaacoub** — 68
Fattet Kafta (Meat Balls with Tomato Sauce and Yoghurt)	70
Karissa bil Tahini (Karissa in Tahini Sauce)	72
Maamoul Bil Raha (Lokoum Maamoul)	74

Safaa Sarkis Shalhoub — 76
Kibbet El Raheb (Monk's Kibbeh)	78
Maacroon Bi Toum (Gnocchis in Garlic Sauce)	80
Moujaddara Bil Burghul (Burghul Lentil Pilaf)	82
Kabakeeb Safarjal (Quince Balls)	84

KFARDEBIANE, Samira Zgheib	86
Shamandar Bil Tahini (Beetroot Salad with Tahini Sauce)	88
Madfouneh (Green Beans with Tomatoes and Rice)	90
Sfouf Bi Debs (Apple Mollasses Cakes)	92
MINIARA, Rose El-Murr	94
Fatayer Areesheh (Milk Curd Turnovers)	96
Mtabbleh (Whole Wheat and Yoghurt)	98
Samkeh Harra Miniariyyeh (Miniara Spicey Baked Fish)	100

THE WEST BEQAA — 102

AIN ZEBDEH, Noha Abi Rached	106
Batata Hamra Bil Taratour (Red Potatoes in Tahini Sauce)	108
Kibbet Batata Bil Qawarma (Potato Kibbeh Stuffed with Labneh and Qawarma)	110
Zinkol	114
Mansoufit Lakteen (Pumpkin Mansouf)	116
Zinkol Bil Laban (Zinkol with Yoghurt)	118
Moufarraket batata (Potato with meat stir fry)	120
AITANITE, Labibeh Al Rassy	122
Kaak El Shaanineh (Palm Sunday Cookies)	124
KHERBET QANAFAR, Lina Haddad	126
Balghassoun (Anchusa Fritters)	130
Dardar A Hommos (Spanish Thistle with Chick Peas)	132
Mainiyyet Bulgur (Wild Jute Mallow)	134
Kibbet Joz (Walnut Kibbeh)	136
Lina's Kibbet Yakteen (Pumpkin Kibbeh)	138
Kibbet Yakteen Bi Kishk (Kishk Soup with Pumpkin Kebbeh)	142
Kaak Bi Haleeb (Easter Cookies)	146
Zalabiet Yakteen (Pumpkin Fritters)	150
KHRAIYZAT, Thérèse Khoury	152
Dardar Mtabbal (Dardar with Lemons and Garlic)	154
Saifi	156
SAGHBINE, Joumana Chedid	158
Tabbouleh Bil Qawarma (Tabbouleh with Qawarma)	160
Zinkol A Hamod (Lemon Zinkol)	162

SHOUF — 164

KHREYBEH, Salim El Ashkar	168
Kibbet Batata Beit El Ashkar (Salim's Potato Kibbeh)	170
Mansoufet Hommos (Chick Pea Mansouf)	172
Tabbouleh Shatawiyyeh (Winter Tabbouleh)	174
Yakhnet El Foul Bil Burghul (Burghul and Fava Bean Stew)	176
Shamahliyyeh Bil Bayd (Yoghurt Poached Eggs)	178

MAASSER EL SHOUF, Elissar Temraz	180
Fatayer Bil Koussa (Courgette Turnovers)	184
Fatayer Bi Yakteen (Pumpkin Turnovers)	186
Makhlouta (Mixed Bean Stew)	188
Shish Barak Bi Sumac (Shish Barak with Sumac)	190
Halawah Lawhiyyeh (Lawhiyyeh Cookies)	192
MROSTI, Bassima Zeidan	194
Hindbeh Bil Labneh (Wild Chicory with Yoghurt Sauce)	196
Mtabbal Yakteen (Pumpkin Tahini Dip)	198
Kibbet Akkoub (Gundelia Kibbeh)	202
Tabbouleh Bil Adass (Lentil Tabbouleh)	206
Tabboulet Ors Anneh (Eryngo Tabbouleh)	208
Maghmourat Misheh (Sautéed Salsify and Chick Peas)	210
Makloubet Akkoub (Gundelia Pilaf)	212
Misheh Bil Qawarma (Salsify with Qawarma)	214

THE SOUTH   216

HASBAYA, Wafaa Shmeiss	220
Kibbet Batata Bil Malfouf (Potato Kibbeh with Cabbage Leaves)	222
Moussakat Batinjen (Lebanese Aubergine Moussaka)	224
Maash (Mung Bean soup)	226
Moughrabiet Djej Bil Khozami (Chicken Moughrabieh with Lavender)	228
Riz Bi Debs (Grape Molasses Rice Pudding)	230
Kaak Bil Khozami (Lavender Cookies)	232
MARJEYOUN, Ferial & Majed Makhoul	234
Adass Bil Shumar (Lentils with Fennel)	236
Brikat (Walnut and Egg Pies)	238
Tabboulet Foul (Fava Bean Tabbouleh)	240
Waraq Enab Bil Djej (Stuffed Courgettes and Vine Leaves with Chicken)	242
ZAWTAR, Imm Qassem & Muhammad Nehme	246
Kammouneh (Fresh Herb Kibbeh Paste)	250
Frakeh (Kibbeh Tartar)	252
Kibbet Banadoura (Tomato Kibbeh)	254
Kibbet Batata Bil Kammouneh (Potatoe Kibbeh with Kammouneh)	256

Glossary	258
Index	259
Contact information	262
Acknowledgements	263

FOREWORD

Everyone thinks they know Lebanese food. And many of us can't live without it. But this book invites us to go further, and experience the hidden culinary treasures of Lebanon's mountains. It gives us an extraordinary window into the lives of the communities that have lived in these distant and beautiful areas for generations. By experiencing their cuisine, we not only remember a way of life. We preserve it for future generations to enjoy. The Lebanese are the world's greatest cooks, and this book reminds us why.

Professor Tom Fletcher CMG
Former UK Ambassador to Lebanon

A JOURNEY OF PRESERVATION

The richly diverse culinary heritage of the Lebanese mountains was one of the most serendipitous discoveries in my "Million Step" journey across these remote peaks.

We buy cookbooks because we either want to know how to cook or we're tired of the recipes we know and are looking for something new. There are a vast amount of choices out there: organic, healthy, fusion, old recipes with a new twist, or little known cuisines, and so much more. But what about the undiscovered recipes, the specialties that are generations old but most people have never heard of? What I came to realize at the end of this journey was that it is about a lot more than just food. It is about heritage, context and the unique combination of social and historical factors that create the very special essence that is Lebanese cuisine.

Lebanon is 210 km long. It is smaller than most states in the USA, yet through a unique and magical combination of cultural exchanges, varying geography and religious influences it has produced a richly diverse culinary heritage that most Lebanese are not fully aware of. But, as I said, it is not just about the food. Discovering these dishes in the villagers' homes was a heartwarming experience because they are naturally generous and welcoming. It is a holistic experience. For me, experiences are not complete and fulfilling unless they are shared. This is part of the reason why I decided to write this book. All these recipes have been handed down from generation to generation orally, and, if not recorded, many may one day be lost.

On the very first day of my 30-day trek on the Lebanon Mountain Trail in 2009 we stayed in the village of Tashea in Akkar, which was home to only 20% of its former inhabitants. As a result of a lack of job opportunities in the region, as well as the absence of educational and medical facilities, families were forced to move away to the cities. This is an all too common problem in many of Lebanon's mountain villages. The need to create job opportunities through sustainable rural development has become crucial and is critical to maintaining mountain life and traditions.

There is hope. Thanks to NGOs like the Lebanon Mountain Trail Association (LMTA) and the Food Heritage Foundation (FHF) at the American University of Beirut (AUB), a new rural eco-tourism industry is evolving.

The LMTA has succeeded in opening economic opportunities in over 30 villages along the trail. A driving force in the development of Lebanon's ecotourism sector, the LMTA has identified, renovated and established nine guesthouses. It has also trained and created a network of over 45 local guides in 27 villages.

Meanwhile, the FHF's mission is to conserve Lebanon's indigenous culinary knowledge through the preservation, documentation and revival of Lebanon's traditional food heritage. By preserving our ancestors' culinary treasures, we ensure a legacy for future generations.

The FHF feels strongly that local food heritage can be a potent tool for economic development. Increasing consumer awareness is vital and will raise public demand for healthy home-cooked local cuisine and produce. To do this, we need to set up strong permanent links between urban and rural communities through which small farmers and producers can raise awareness of their culinary and agricultural traditions and sell their products directly to consumers. The foundation works closely with the Environment and Sustainable Development Unit at the American University of Beirut to further this cause. It is with their cooperation and with the guidance of the FHF that I embarked on this culinary adventure. I hope it enriches both your kitchen and your understanding of Lebanon. It did mine.

Hana El-Hibri

Beirut, April 2nd, 2019

ON THE WILD SIDE

Balghassoun, misheh, herrak, saifi, dardar… I had never heard of these plants before setting out to discover the treasures that lie in the culinary heritage of the mountains. These are all edible wild plants that constitute a significant part of the diet in many of our mountain villages. Seasonal foraging is part of a way of life, a way of life that is in touch with the land and in tune with its natural cycles. People intuitively recognize the subtle signs that signal the imminent sprouting of the many wild plants. "When grape leaves are smaller than the palm of your hand, it is time to go forage for akkoub," Bassima from Mrosti tells me.

The knowledge of the precious health benefits of each plant has been handed down from generation to generation. Preservation of this knowledge, like many aspects of our culinary heritage, is invaluable.

The method of cleaning, prepping and cooking is particular to each plant. Some require blanching, others not. Wherever possible, I offer alternatives to the ingredients that are uncommon or hard to find, but for many of the wild edible plants there are no substitutes. Finding the English or Latin name of these plants is still a work in progress – something that the Food Heritage Foundation is working on - so sometimes I only offer the Arabic name. I suspect many of these plants are endemic to Lebanon.

LATIN AND ENGLISH NAMES OF WILD EDIBLE PLANTS

ARABIC	ENGLISH	LATIN
Akkoub	Gundelia	Gundelia tournefortii
Balghassoun	Italian Bugloss	Anchusa azurea
Dardar	Spanish Thistle	Centaurea hyalolepis
Hendbeh	Wild Chicory	Cichorium intybus
Herka or Herrak	Water Cress	Nasturtium officinale
Hommaïda	Curled Dock	Rumex crispus
Korrat	Wild Leeks	Allium ampeloprasum
Khebaïzeh	Mallow	Malva sylvestris
Korra	Water Parsnip	Helosciadium nodiflorum
Mainiyyeh	Wild Jute Mallow	Celosia argentea
Mesheh	Salsify	Tragopogon buphtalmoides
Ors Anni	Eryngo	Eryngium creticum

Some of the ingredients in this book, such as a lot of the edible wild plants, are not readily available in supermarkets, but over the last 15 years, in the wake of an awareness and appreciation for the value of going back to simple, organic and traditional food options, there has been a revival of the Farmers' Market concept in Beirut. Initiatives, like Kamal Mouzawak's Souk El Tayeb, provide local family-run farms and artisanal producers with a way to bring their goods to the heart of the capital on Saturdays, while through the week Beirutis can also access several other markets such as the Badaro Urban Market and the Food Heritage Foundation's Souk Al Souk. These offer, in addition to home grown and homemade products, foraged plants and herbs along with honey and mouneh (see glossary) and other ingredients that can be hard to find.

"Cuisine is the most sincere and authentic expression of our identity. It is the one aspect of our culture and traditions that is the most easily shared and travels the most effortlessly through time and space. The over 12 million Lebanese immigrants living abroad have one aspect of their heritage in common that they all took with them: Lebanese cuisine."

Kamal Mouzawak
Founder, Souk El Tayeb

THE NORTH

THE NORTH
ANDQET

HANA SHAAR

"It's the one that looks like a children's playhouse," Sleiman Shaar points out, directing us to his colourful home, a building that is hard to miss and one that exudes a lighthearted vibe that makes guests feel at home.

His wife, Hana, is cooking up a storm in the kitchen. The positive energy emanating from her smile is contagious and almost palpable. Her love for cooking is reflected in the care and joy with which she handles the food. Perhaps the remoteness of this town may explain why the specialties Hana will be preparing today are unique to Andqet even if she has added her own touch to these generations old recipes – pomegranate seeds to the Jermesh, a touch of chilli powder to the Kibbeh Bil Adass Wal Shumar. She adds her *"nafass"*, breath, to everything she prepares.

"They call us the crazy couple," Hana tells me, smiling. People could not understand how they could continue to smile and laugh knowing the adversity they have faced. During the civil war, she lost her job as an elementary school supervisor and Sleiman suffered a drastic wage cut as a French teacher. With three young children, they lived pretty much hand to mouth, farming and taking whatever jobs they could. She is also candid about her bout of cancer, her smile a reflection of her defiant love for life in the face of this disease. I understand now why Sleiman and her son Samer hover around her protectively.

The father and son are now working together to expand their pomegranate molasses business. Pomegranates have historically been a main crop in the far North and find their way into many regional recipes.

In her quest to find alternative ways to make an income, Hana taught herself how to sew. She also went to a craft school and even learnt how to make false teeth. But the quest ended with cooking. "If I can cook all day and love what I am doing, why would I do anything else?" she beams.

FALL, WINTER **MAIN DISHES**
MAKES: 24

جرميش
JERMESH

2½ cups/560g burghul (bulgur wheat), fine
¾ cups/90g plain flour
500g onion, finely chopped
1 large bunch fresh mint, finely chopped
½ tsp chilli paste
½ tsp ground black pepper
salt, to taste
1 pomegranate, seeded

1. Cover the burghul with water in a large bowl with 1 cm water over the burghul and soak for 30 minutes. Add all the other ingredients except the pomegranate seeds. Knead into a dough. When well mixed gently incorporate the pomegranate seeds into the dough. Make into small balls that fit in the palm of a hand.

2. Preheat a medium sized frying pan. Lightly oil.

3. To make the patties cut two pieces of greaseproof paper into 30 centimeter squares. On a flat surface, place a ball of dough in the centre of the greaseproof paper. Flatten the ball of dough with the palm of your hand. Place the second piece of wax paper on top. Flatten with a rolling pin into a thin circle of around a centimetre thick. Remove the top piece of greaseproof paper and turn the patty over into a hot frying pan. Peel off the greaseproof paper. Repeat this process with each ball of dough.

4. Cook until the bottom of the patty is well browned. Flip over and cook until the other side is well browned. Place on a serving dish. Just before serving, brush each patty with a little bit of olive oil.

DIFFICULTY: ★

•KIBBEH   •PASTRIES   •STEWS   •SWEETS   •TABBOULEH   •VEGAN   •VEGETARIAN   •WHEAT FREE   •WILD EDIBLE PLANTS

SPRING **APPETIZERS, SIDE DISHES**

MAKES: 36

كبه بالعدس والشومر
KIBBEH BIL ADDASS WAL SHUMAR
LENTIL AND FENNEL KEBBEH

KIBBEH DOUGH

3 cups/675g burghul (bulgur wheat), fine
1 cup/120g plain flour
½ tsp dried basil
½ tsp dried marjoram
½ tsp dried mint
¼ tsp chilli powder
1 onion, grated

FILLING

1½ cups/300g whole brown lentils
½kg onions, chopped
2 tbsp vegetable oil
1 large bunch fresh mint
1 large bunch fresh fennel leaves
½ tsp baking powder
salt, to taste

1. To make the kibbeh dough add water to the burghul to so it is just covered (by about 1cm) in a large bowl. Soak for 30 minutes. Add the remaining dough ingredients and knead until malleable. If it is too stiff add a little more water.

2. For the filling put the lentils into a pan and cover with water. Bring to the boil and lower the heat. Cook until well done. Drain the lentils. Add the onions and oil to a large pan and sauté over a medium heat until golden. Add all the herbs and spices to the pan and mix well. Add the cooked lentils and lower the heat. Cook for 5 minutes, or until the fennel is done.

3. Make kibbehs according to the method on page 140.

4. Bring a deep pan of water to the boil. Add salt. Carefully drop the kibbeh balls into the boiling water. Cook them in the boiling water on a high heat for 1 minute. Remove from the pan with a slotted spoon and place in a colander to cool. When cooled deep fry the kibbeh balls until golden. Place on paper towels on a plate to absorb any excess oil.

NOTES

Hana recommends eating these kibbehs with a simple wild chicory salad on the side.

DIFFICULTY: ★★★

•KIBBEH •PASTRIES •STEWS •SWEETS •TABBOULEH •VEGAN •VEGETARIAN •WHEAT FREE •WILD EDIBLE PLANTS

ALL SEASON **DESSERTS**
MAKES: 20

قراص قمح
KRASS QAMEH

This is traditionally made for Christmas and Epiphany

KIBBEH DOUGH

8 cups/1kg flour
2 tsp fenugreek powder
3 tsp fennel powder
3 tsp anis powder
½ cup/125ml vegetable oil
1 tsp dried yeast
1½ cups/375ml water
½ cup/100g sugar

3 cups/600g granulated sugar
4 cups/1l hot milk

1. In a large mixing bowl, mix all the dry ingredients and knead together with the oil and water. Cover and leave to rise in a warm place for a minimum of 3 hours. Divide into small balls and place on trays. Cover and leave to rise for another 2 hours.

2. Preheat the oven to 220°C/450°F/gas mark 7. Line two baking trays with greaseproof paper. Flatten the dough balls onto the mould. Remove from the mould and place, pattern side up, onto trays. Or shape the dough balls into cookie shapes if moulds unavailable. Bake until both sides are lightly browned, turning them halfway through cooking (after about ten minutes). Mix the milk and 3 cups/600g sugar in a pan. Bring to the boil. Puncture the cakes with a fork three or four times. Dip each cookie into the hot milk and sugar with a slotted spoon for two minutes. Remove and place on a serving platter. Serve warm.

DIFFICULTY: ★★

•KIBBEH   •PASTRIES   •STEWS   •SWEETS   •TABBOULEH   •VEGAN   •VEGETARIAN   •WHEAT FREE   •WILD EDIBLE PLANTS

THE NORTH
ASSIA

SANA JABBOUR

"This type of clay pot is the first cooking vessel that was used by man," Sana tells me. "It came before the use of metal, so it is tens of thousands of years old." They have been making them in Assia for generations and unlike other Lebanese pottery, in Assia it is exclusively a women's craft, handed down from mother to daughter. When Sana's mother, Heneineh, joins us for lunch, she fondly recollects how, at the age of ten, her mother gave her little tasks while working on the clay. "It was her way of keeping me out of mischief," she says with a twinkle in her crystal blue eyes.

All the materials used to make the pots come from the surrounding area. It is a mixture of a special clay and a certain type of rock crystal that lends the pots their heat preserving properties. The pots are hand built, not wheel thrown, and no glaze is used or needed. In the 19th and 20th centuries, over 75% of the inhabitants of Assia were potters. Taking their wares on donkeys, they would travel to barter for grains and other much-needed staples.

Sana is famous for her Mattmoura, an ingenious crockpot-cum-pressure cooker fire pit technique. During the winter months, when there are a lot of coals used in the wood burning stoves, people would dig a shallow pit, half fill it with coals, put the food-filled mattmoura pot on the coals, and cover it with more coals. This method gives the food a special slow cooked quality with subtle caramelisation. Cooking times vary depending on conditions, outside temperature, heat and the quantity of coal.

ESSENTIALS FOR MAKING ASSIA CLAY POTS

ABOVE

1–3. Hand ground rock crystals.
4. The special local clay that has exceptional firing properties.
5. Water.
6. Knowledge of the centuries–old techniques, handed down through generations.

RIGHT
Firing pots the old-fashioned way.

Sana hand building a clay pot

ALL SEASON MAIN DISHES

SERVES: 6

مطبسه

MTABBSSEH
ZINKOL WITH ONIONS

DOUGH

4 cups/120g plain flour
2 cups/450g burghul (bulgur wheat), fine
½ tsp seven spices
1 tsp cumin

SAUCE

2kg onions, sliced
1 cup/250ml olive oil
1kg tomatoes, chopped
½ tsp cumin powder
½ tsp seven spices
1 tsp marjoram
4 tbsp tomato puree
1 cup/250ml water

1. To make the dough, soak the burghul in ¾ cup/180ml water for 20 minutes in a large bowl until soft. Add all the remaining dough ingredients and knead together to form a dough. Shape the dough into 3cm patties (see opposite).

2. Drop the patties into a large pan of boiling salted water. The discs will float when done – approximately 10 minutes. Drain in a colander and leave to cool.

3. To make the sauce, fry the onions in a pan over a medium heat in the olive oil until golden. Add the tomatoes and spices. Cook for a further 20 minutes. Add the tomato purée and water, stir and cook for another 15 minutes.

4. In a bowl gently toss the patties with a drizzle of olive oil. Add to the sauce and cook for another 10 minutes, stirring carefully.

DIFFICULTY: ★★★

•KIBBEH   •PASTRIES   •STEWS   •SWEETS   •TABBOULEH   •VEGAN   •VEGETARIAN   •WHEAT FREE   •WILD EDIBLE PLANTS

WINTER MAIN DISHES

SERVES: 8

مطمورة

MATTMOURA
SLOW COOKED
CLAY BAKED CHICKEN

2½kg chicken pieces, thighs, drumsticks and breasts

3 onions, quartered

1 head garlic, separated into cloves

1 tsp seven spices

¾ cup hosrum (grape molasses)

½ cup pomegranate molasses

1 lemon, quartered

½ tsp cinnamon powder

½ tsp white pepper powder

2 tsp paprika

½ cup olive oil

1 tsp salt

a little flour and water to make a strip of dough

1. Score the chicken pieces. Place the chicken pieces into a large bowl and sprinkle the spices onto the pieces. Add the hosrum and pomegranate molasses and rub into the chicken pieces. Add the lemon quarters. Marinate for a minimum of 3 hours (overnight is recommended).

2. Light some coals and fan until there are glowing embers. Dig a small shallow pit (a bit larger than the clay pot) and place half the coals in the bottom. Save the rest of the coals to cover the pot.

3. Place everything in the clay pot. Make a small ball of dough out of flour and water. Roll it out into a long thin strip. Cover the pot with the lid. Seal the pot with the dough. Place the pot on top of the coals. Cover with the remaining coals. Depending on the strength of the coals the chicken should take between 3 and 4 hours. To test whether the chicken is cooked through, remove the pastry stopper from the lid and insert a long skewer to test the chicken. When the chicken is done, remove the pot from the coals. Remove the stopper from the lid to let any steam escape. Break the dough seal and open the lid. Serve straight from the pot.

NOTES

You can substitute the chicken with any kind of roasting meat.

You can substitute the clay pot for a cast iron pot. Cook in a low heat oven instead of fire pit cooking. But for the authentic flavour nothing beats the original method.

DIFFICULTY: ★★

•KIBBEH •PASTRIES •STEWS •SWEETS •TABBOULEH •VEGAN •VEGETARIAN •WHEAT FREE •WILD EDIBLE PLANTS

The first pressure cooker. Fire pit, clay pot with pressure valve feature. The ancient method of fire pit cooking dates back over 200,000 years. Harnessing fire by using a fire pit was a huge leap in the development of every culture in the world

THE NORTH
AQOURA

GUITTA & PHILIPPE GERMANOS

HERITAGE AND HOSPITALITY IN AQOURA

Nestled in a grove of mature oak trees, surrounded by apple, cherry and plum orchards, the tastefully-renovated old stone guesthouse, run by mother and son team Guitta and Philippe Germanos, affords stunning views overlooking the valley of the Adonis river.

Philippe used to work for a tech multinational but decided to abandon his career to return to his family estate in Aqoura, a move that was driven by a desire for a simpler life and the need to return to his land and preserve his heritage. But he never abandoned the spirit of entrepreneurship that he inherited from his parents and he soon set about re-cultivating his family's orchard, offering agro-tourism activities such as cherry and apple picking. Then the Lebanon Mountain Trail Association approached him with the idea of becoming an official guesthouse for the trail. The Bed & Bloom guesthouse, steeped in generations of family history and tradition and full of memories and heirlooms, was born.

Guitta, sitting on a diwan in her garden, reminds me that in the 19th and early 20th centuries, at the height of the silk industry, which at the time represented 50% of Mount Lebanon's economy, the orchards were planted mainly with mulberry trees. When the silk industry collapsed due to the introduction of competing Chinese products to Europe, it caused one of the biggest exoduses in Lebanon's history, with many of the area's inhabitants seeking a better life abroad, particularly in the Americas.

But Philip's great-grandfather had vision and resilience. Instead of leaving, he planted his orchards with apples, two varieties of which - Golden and Starking - he brought back from Italy and, through careful grafting, eventually adapted to Lebanon's mountainous conditions. Apples are now one of Lebanon's main cash crops for both the local and export markets.

APPLE SYRUP

Guitta noticed that a lot of apples that were perfectly good, but just not very pretty, were going to waste because they did not meet the market standards. She wanted to find a use for them other than vinegar and created her own apple syrup using the grape syrup model. She uses it now as a sugar substitute in most of her recipes. It has a unique taste that is a bit tart with a caramel flavor. Today, she is working with other apple farmers in Aqoura to make apple syrup on a larger, more economically-viable scale.

ALL SEASON SIDE DISHES

SERVES: 10

بطاطا بالجوز
BATATA BIL JOZ
WALNUT MASHED POTATOES

6 medium potatoes, boiled and peeled
¾ cups/100g walnuts
3 onions, peeled
⅛ tsp white pepper powder
salt, to taste
⅛ tsp black pepper powder
2 tbsp olive oil

1. Grate one onion and quarter the other two.

2. Place the warm potatoes in a large bowl and blend with a hand blender until smooth and creamy. Then add the walnuts (saving a few to garnish the dish at the end) and grated onion. Add the spices, olive oil and salt. Knead well and serve in shallow platter. Decorate with a few whole walnuts and the quartered onions. Serve with olive oil on the side.

DIFFICULTY: ★

•KIBBEH •PASTRIES •STEWS •SWEETS •TABBOULEH •VEGAN •VEGETARIAN •WHEAT FREE •WILD EDIBLE PLANTS

SPRING, SUMMER **SIDE DISHES**

SERVES: 4

سلطة قرّه و جرجير
SLATET KORRA WA JARJEER
WATER PARSNIP AND ROCKET SALAD

2 cups/50g water parsnip
2 cups/50g rocket
1 white onion, sliced

DRESSING
¼ cup/60ml olive oil
¼ cup/60ml apple vinegar
1 tbsp yoghurt
a pinch of white pepper powder
salt, to taste

1. Wash the water parsnip and rocket thoroughly. Drain in a colander. Chop and toss in a large bowl.

2. Put all the dressing ingredients in a glass jar. Tighten the lid and shake until homogeneous. Add desired amount to salad and toss well. Serve in a salad bowl.

NOTES
The dressing can keep for 2 weeks in the refrigerator. There is no substitute for water parsnip – a wild, edible plant.

DIFFICULTY: ★

•KIBBEH   •PASTRIES   •STEWS   •SWEETS   •TABBOULEH   •VEGAN   •VEGETARIAN   •WHEAT FREE   •WILD EDIBLE PLANTS

ALL SEASON **MAIN DISHES**
SERVES: 4

معكرون بلبنه وقورما
MAACROON BI LABNEH WA QAWARMA
GNOCCHIS IN YOGHURT AND QAWARMA

2 cups/240g plain flour
1 cup/250ml water
salt, to taste
1 cup/225g labneh
   (see page 196)
1 garlic clove, crushed
½ tsp dried mint
¼ cup/60g qawarma

1. To make the dough, mix the flour, salt and water in a large bowl and work into a hard dough. Divide the dough into 8 portions and place in a well-floured bowl. Roll each piece into a 1cm thick strip. Cut the strip into 1cm long segments. Press and roll each piece.

2. In a bowl mix the labneh, garlic and mint. Set aside.

3. Sauté the qawarma until browned.

4. Bring 8 cups/2l of water to a boil. Gently drop the dough pieces into the boiling water. Cook for approximately 5 minutes or until the pasta dough is cooked (al dente). Remove with a slotted spoon and add to the labneh mixture, saving some of the cooking liquid. Mix the pasta pieces gently with the labneh. The sauce should have a creamy consistency. If it is too dry, add a little bit of the cooking water. Transfer to a serving bowl.

5. When ready to serve add the qawarma on top.

NOTES
Qawarma may be substituted with minced beef.

DIFFICULTY: ★★★★

•KIBBEH   •PASTRIES   •STEWS   •SWEETS   •TABBOULEH   •VEGAN   •VEGETARIAN   •WHEAT FREE   •WILD EDIBLE PLANTS

ALL SEASON **MAIN DISHES**
SERVES: 6

طبيّبيسه
TBAYBISSEH

2½ cups/300g plain flour
300g pumpkin, peeled and cut
1¼ cups/300g burghul (bulgur wheat)
2 tbsp dried mint
1 tsp salt
¼ tsp seven spices
3 large onions
1 cup/240ml sunflower oil
8 cups/2l water
2 tbsp debs hosrum

1. Boil the pumpkin until very soft. Drain and reserve the cooking liquid.

2. To make the tbaybisseh dough, put the burghul in a large mixing bowl. Put the boiled pumpkin pieces on top and leave to stand for 5 minutes. Grate one of the onions and add to the pumpkin/burghul mixture with the spices, mint and flour. Knead all the ingredients together to form a stiff dough. If too dry and crumbly, gradually add some of the pumpkin cooking liquid. The dough should be homogeneous. Shape the dough into 2cm wide patties. Place on a baking tray in a single layer so they don't stick to each other.

3. Slice the two remaining onions. Fry the onions in the sunflower oil in a frying pan over a medium heat until golden brown. Remove the onions from the oil with a slotted spoon and place on paper towels on a plate to absorb any excess oil. Set aside.

4. Bring the water to a boil. Gently drop the tbaybisseh discs into the boiling water. Cook for approximately 5 minutes, stirring occasionally. The dough is done when the discs float to the surface. Drain in a colander, reserving some of the liquid. Return to the pan and add the fried onions and the debs hosrum. Add one cup of the cooking liquid and simmer for 10 to 15 minutes, until the sauce thickens. Serve in a deep dish.

NOTES
Debs hosrum can be substituted with reduced balsamic vinegar.

DIFFICULTY: ★★

•KIBBEH •PASTRIES •STEWS •SWEETS •TABBOULEH •VEGAN •VEGETARIAN •WHEAT FREE •WILD EDIBLE PLANTS

THE NORTH
BQAA SEFRINE

IMM MAJED

BUILD AND THEY WILL COME!

Three days into my "A Million Steps" journey across Lebanon's mountains I fell ill. Since I could not hike that day, I was driven to the next village of Beqaa Sefrine to wait for my team. It was the first year that Imm and Abou Majed were receiving guests in their 3-bedroom guesthouse. They welcomed me and took care of me, a stranger, with so much genuine warmth and generosity, I was truly taken aback. As a Beiruti, I have always wished to have a mountain village that I too could call home. Now, nine years later, whenever I return to Beqaa Sefrine I am received like a long-lost daughter.

On our early walk through the village, Imm Majed points out the different crops her family cultivates. The tall mature wild rose trees have deep roots, as does her family. Rosewater is a typical *mouneh* (preserve) product of the area. Abou Majed and his son Majed have been building additions since they realized that guesthouses were becoming a profitable enterprise. They have added two more apartments in addition to the house I stayed in nine years ago, doing all the work, aside from the electricity and plumbing, entirely themselves.

They also built a shed that Imm Majed uses as an outdoor kitchen and where she stores all her *mouneh* on floor to ceiling shelves. Food has a habit of bringing people together in many ways. Imm Majed's outdoor kitchen is where the family comes together to cook, eat and pray.

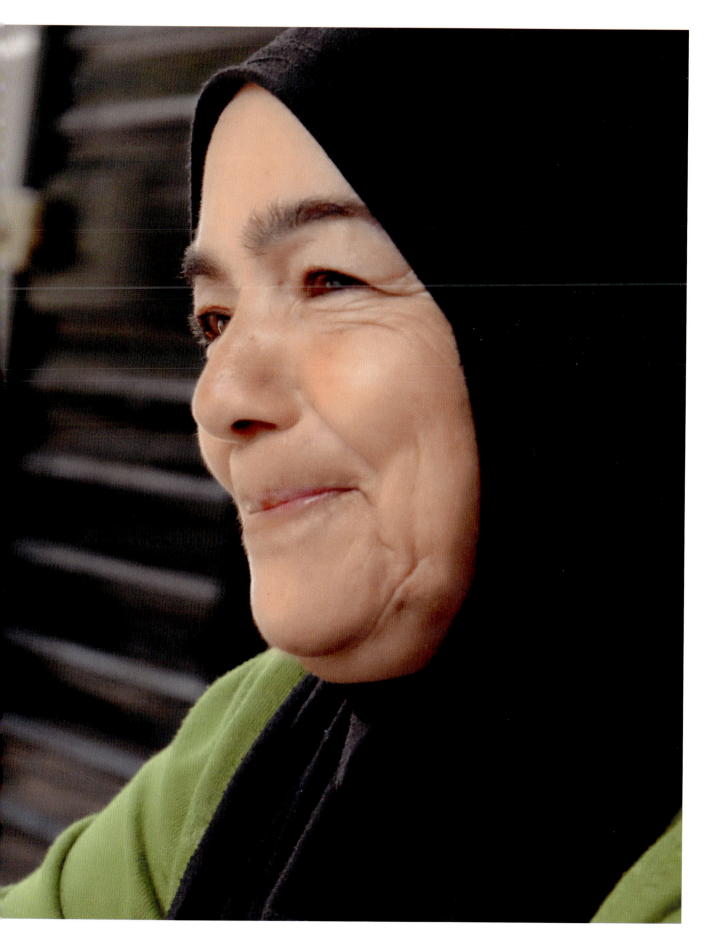

SUMMER APPETIZERS
MAKES: 40

فطاير بالسلق و الجوز

FATAYER BIL SILIQ WA JOZ
SWISS CHARD AND WALNUT TURNOVERS

DOUGH
8 cups/1kg flour
½ tsp dried yeast
pinch salt
1 egg
½ cup/120ml vegetable oil
water

FILLING
2kg Swiss chard, washed and chopped into medium-sized ribbons
1½ cups/150g walnuts, chopped
1½ tsp sumac
½kg onions, chopped
⅓ cup/113g pomegranate molasses

1. To make the dough, mix all the dry ingredients in a large bowl. Add the egg and oil and knead together. Add a little water until the dough is firm but still malleable. Knead the dough into a large ball and place in a floured bowl. Cover and leave the dough to rest for at least an hour.

2. Dust a work surface with flour. Make small dough balls of approximately 2cm in diameter. Place on the work surface and cover with a clean, damp dishcloth to prevent it drying out.

3. For the filling lightly oil two baking trays. Mix all the filling ingredients in a bowl. Flatten each dough ball into a thin disc. Using a teaspoon, spoon some filling into the centre of each disc. Bring up the sides of the dough discs and seal by pressing to form a triangle. (See photo on facing page).

4. Bake at 180°C till browned.

NOTES
If filling begins to get watery, place in a sieve to avoid turnovers breaking open during cooking.

DIFFICULTY: ★★★

•KIBBEH   •PASTRIES   •STEWS   •SWEETS   •TABBOULEH   •VEGAN   •VEGETARIAN   •WHEAT FREE   •WILD EDIBLE PLANTS

SPRING, SUMMER **APPETIZERS, SIDE DISHES**

SERVES: 8

سلق باللوبيا
SILIQ BIL LOUBIYEH
SWISS CHARD WITH GREEN BEANS

1 bunch Swiss chard, thoroughly washed
1 cup/170g black eyed peas, soaked overnight
2 onions, chopped
¼ cup/125ml olive oil
1 bunch coriander, chopped
1 garlic clove, crushed
1 lemon, freshly squeezed
¼ tsp black pepper powder
⅛ tsp chilli paste
½ tsp salt

1. Separate the leaves from the stalks of the Swiss chard. Chop the stalks and ¼ of the leaves into 1cm pieces. Save the remaining ¾ of the leaves for another dish such as fatayer bil siliq.

2. Boil the beans until soft. Drain and set aside.

3. In a large pan fry the onions in the olive oil over a medium heat until golden. Add the garlic and coriander and stir for one minute. Add the chard and beans to the pan and cook for a further 5 minutes.

4. Mix in the lemon juice, black pepper, salt and chilli paste.

DIFFICULTY: ★★

•KIBBEH   •PASTRIES   •STEWS   •SWEETS   •TABBOULEH   •VEGAN   •VEGETARIAN   •WHEAT FREE   •WILD EDIBLE PLANTS

SPRING, SUMMER **APPETIZERS, SIDE DISHES**

SERVES: 8

كوسى متبّل
KOUSSA MTABBAL
SAUTEED COURGETTES

2 onions, chopped
¼ cup/60ml olive oil
3 garlic cloves, chopped
3 green peppers, diced
500g courgettes, diced
1 tbsp tomato puree
2 tomatoes, diced
⅒ tsp chilli paste
¼ tsp black pepper powder
¼ tsp seven spices

In a large pan sauté the onion in the oil over a medium heat until golden. Add the garlic and sauté for another minute. Add the courgettes and peppers. Cook until half done – around 10-15 minutes (still a bit crunchy). Add all the remaining ingredients and cook for another 5 minutes stirring occasionally.

DIFFICULTY: ★

•KIBBEH •PASTRIES •STEWS •SWEETS •TABBOULEH •VEGAN •VEGETARIAN •WHEAT FREE •WILD EDIBLE PLANTS

ALL SEASON **MAIN DISHES**

SERVES: 10

شيشبرك مع مدردره

SHISH BARAK MA MOUDARDARA
GOAT YOGHURT SHISH BARAK WITH LENTIL PILAF

DOUGH
1kg flour
2 cup/500ml water
1 tbsp salt

FILLING
500g minced lamb (can be substituted with beef)
3 onions, chopped
¼ tsp black pepper powder
¼ tbsp seven spices

MOUDARDARA
2 onions, chopped
½ cup/125ml sunflower oil
1 tsp salt
6 cups/1½l water
2 cups/400g brown lentils
2 cups/370g American rice (long grain rice)
1 onion, sliced

COOKED YOGHURT
2½l goat yoghurt (can be substituted with cow yoghurt)
1 tbsp cornflour
½ cup/125ml water
1 large bunch coriander, washed and chopped
3 garlic cloves, crushed

1. To make the dough mix all the dough ingredients and knead by hand. The dough should be firm and not sticky. Cover and set aside.

2. For the filling sauté the onions in a pan over a low heat until soft. Add the meat and cook until browned. Add the spices and cook for another minute.

3. To make the moudardara fry the onions in the oil over a medium heat in a large pan until golden. Pour in the water and boil for 15 minutes. Add the lentils and cook for about 20 minutes until soft. Then mix in the rice and salt and bring to the boil. Lower the heat and cook until done, approximately 20 minutes. In a separate pan fry the sliced onion until brown. Place on paper towels to absorb excess oil and set aside to garnish the moudardara when served.

4. To make the shish barak dust a work surface with flour and roll out the dough until it is thin. Using a small coffee cup (4-6cm diameter), cut out small circles.
1. Place a small amount of the filling in the centre of each cut out dough circle (about a teaspoon). 2. Fold over and firmly close to make a half circle. 3. Press both tips together. (See following pages for guidance).

5. Dissolve the cornflour in the ½ cup of water. Place the yoghurt into a pan and stir in the dissolved cornflour and water. Cook over a medium heat until the yoghurt thickens. Lower the heat and cook for an additional 20 minutes stirring constantly.

6. Carefully drop the shish barak balls into the boiling yoghurt. Cook until al dente, stirring occasionally. Fry the garlic and fresh coriander for 1 minute in the olive oil. Add to the yoghurt just before serving.

7. Place the moudardara in a tureen or deep bowl and carefully pour the yoghurt and shish barak mixture over the top. Garnish with the fried onions.

DIFFICULTY: ★★★★

•KIBBEH   •PASTRIES   •STEWS   •SWEETS   •TABBOULEH   •VEGAN   •VEGETARIAN   •WHEAT FREE   •WILD EDIBLE PLANTS

SHISH BARAK STEPS

THE NORTH
BAINO

SAMIA & MARWAN NAUFAL

TALES OF ACORNS AND STEWS

The massive oak overshadows Baino's town square and Marwan Naufal's generations-old family restaurant. The land on which the restaurant sits once belonged to a certain Yaacoub Farah, whose two sons were drafted into the army during the days of the Ottoman empire and shipped off to Turkey. Their father was heartbroken and the boys weren't happy either. They deserted and walked all the way back to Lebanon, penniless and surviving on acorns. When they finally made it back home, they still had a few acorns left in their pockets, one of which was planted and grew to become the town landmark.

In 1914, Marwan's father rented the small piece of land and opened a little coffee shop. The villagers soon started gathering at his modest little café, drawn in not only by his freshly ground coffee but also in his talent for storytelling. Marwan has the same ability to captivate with his witty storytelling.

This one is about his signature specialty dish: Lahm Bil Khal (meat and vinegar stew). "This story is set at the same time as that of Yaacoub Farah and his sons. There was a poor man from Beirut who took the opportunity to work in the household of an Ottoman Pasha in Turkey. He ended up in the kitchen assisting the cook. Soon he mastered the Pasha's favorite dish: Lahm Bil Khal. When the Pasha passed away, since the man had no children, he was forced to return to Beirut where he decided to open a modest little restaurant on El Bourj, Beirut's busy central square, where his speciality was Lahm Bil Khal. One day, by chance, a wealthy merchant from Baino called Dawoud Naufal passed by the little restaurant and decided to try his unusual dish. He loved it so much he would stop by every time he was in the city. Finally, one day he made the man an offer: "Come with me to Baino. I will double what you are making here and provide you with a home and schooling for your children. All I want is that you become my cook and make me Lahm Bil Khal whenever I want it."

Today, people still seek out Marwan Naufal's restaurant, Naufalieh, for the signature dish, that, as far as we know, is only made in Baino.

SUMMER, FALL **APETIZERS, SIDE DISHES**

SERVES: 6

باذنحان مقلي

BATINJAN MIKLI
LOW OIL FRIED EGGPLANT

2 aubergines
salt to taste
2 cups/500ml vegetable oil
2 tbsp pomegranate molasses

1. In a large bowl of water add salt at a ratio of 1 tbsp per litre to make the brine. Peel the aubergines and slice lengthwise into 1cm thick slices. Cut each slice in half. Put the cut slices in the water and soak overnight or for 24 hours if possible.

2. Remove the aubergine slices from the water. Pat dry with a clean dishcloth. Deep fry in hot oil until browned. Place on paper towels on a plate to absorb any excess oil. Serve on a shallow serving dish and drizzle with pomegranate molasses.

NOTES
Soaking the eggplant in salted water overnight prevents the eggplant from absorbing oil during deep frying. The result is fried eggplant that is yummy but that is very light and not oily.

DIFFICULTY: ★

•KIBBEH   •PASTRIES   •STEWS   •SWEETS   •TABBOULEH   **•VEGAN**   **•VEGETARIAN**   **•WHEAT FREE**   •WILD EDIBLE PLANTS

ALL SEASON **MAIN DISHES, SIDE DISHES**

MAKES: 20

KIBBEH BAWABNEH

KIBBEH DOUGH

1kg srayseerah

1kg plain flour

1 cup/250ml water

2 onions, finely chopped

1 large bunch fresh mint, finely chopped

1 large bunch fresh parsley, finely chopped

¼ tsp black pepper

¼ tsp chilli paste

FILLING

2kg onions, sliced

2½ tbsp pomegranate molasses

2 tbsp vegetable oil

1. To make the kibbeh dough, mix the flour with the srayseerah in a bowl. Gradually add water until dough is a firm paste – a little bit at a time. Mix in the remaining ingredients. Shape into palm size balls (approximately 5cm in diameter).

2. To make the filling fry the onions over a medium heat until golden. In a bowl, mix the onions with the pomegranate molasses.

3. Place each ball between 2 pieces of plastic and flatten evenly until about 1 cm thick. Spoon about 1 tbsp of filling onto the centre of a patty. Cover with another patty and press perimeter to seal. Press cutter onto patties to clean and reserve surplus for reuse. Dip fingers in water and run along outside to smooth. Repeat until all the dough balls are used.

4. Pre-heat the grill.

5. Lightly brush both sides of each patty with a little vegetable oil and grill on each side until there are brown char marks visible. Serve warm or at room temperature.

NOTES

You can use any round plastic container or a glass ramekin instead of the pastry cutter.

DIFFICULTY: ★★★

•KIBBEH •PASTRIES •STEWS •SWEETS •TABBOULEH •VEGAN •VEGETARIAN •WHEAT FREE •WILD EDIBLE PLANTS

WINTER **MAIN DISHES**
SERVES: 10

لحم بخل

LAHM BI KHAL
MEAT IN VINEGAR SAUCE

500g beef cubes
500g quince, peeled and cut into cubes
500g chayote, peeled and cut into cubes
300g carrots, peeled and cut in 1cm pieces
250g pearl onions, peeled
250g garlic, peeled
½ cup/125ml water
½ cu/125ml grape vinegar
¼ cup/60ml vegetable oil

1. Brown the beef cubes until half done, around 10 minutes. Set aside.

2. Deep fry the different vegetables separately until they are slightly browned. Place on paper towels in a colander to absorb any excess oil.

3. In a deep pot layer all of the ingredients in the following order: meat, quince, chayote, carrots, onions, garlic.
Add the water and vinegar and bring to the boil. Lower the heat and cook for 15 minutes without stirring.

4. Drain any excess liquid into a bowl. Turn upside-down onto a flat platter to serve.

NOTES
Lahm Bil Khal is traditionally served accompanied by Kibbeh Bawabneh (see previous page).

DIFFICULTY: ★

•KIBBEH •PASTRIES •STEWS •SWEETS •TABBOULEH •VEGAN •VEGETARIAN •WHEAT FREE •WILD EDIBLE PLANTS

hayote, also known as mirliton squash, is a light green pear-shaped squash

DOUMA

Diwan Al Baik's garden

The peaceful streets of Douma - a window into a time past, but a way of life that is present.

THE NORTH
DOUMA

GUITTA YAACOUB

The village of Douma is famous for its traditional Lebanese architecture. A walk through its famous market - or souk – offers a window into a way of life that has been shaped by a long history. Guitta Yaacoub's restaurant, Talaya, named after the Canaanite goddess of mist and rain, and which, until a few years ago, was her generations-old family home, stands in the town square. A group of ladies, sitting on the spacious terrace under the shade of the large quince tree, chat away about nothing in particular, as one does in town squares.

Guitta is also an agri-engineer and was manager of the St. Jacob duck farm, but she has always stayed close to her roots and continues to offer unique Douma specialities at Talaya. She has combined traditional maamoul with the locally produced lokoum (Douma was the home of the only lokoum factory in Lebanon) and came up with her specialty Maamoul Bil Raha. Maamoul are usually stuffed with nuts or dates, but the irrepressibly creative Guitta saw the potential for this delicious combination, proving that culinary heritage is dynamic and continually evolving.

ALL SEASON **MAIN DISHES**

SERVES: 8

فتّة كفته

FATTET KAFTA
MEAT BALLS WITH TOMATO
SAUCE AND YOGHURT

MEATBALLS
1kg onions, finely chopped
1kg minced lamb
1 tsp white pepper powder
½ tsp black pepper powder
½ cup/15g fresh parsley, chopped
3 tsp salt
2 tbsp sunflower oil

TOMATO SAUCE
1½kg onions, sliced
1 cup/250ml sunflower oil
2 cinnamon sticks
1 bay leaf
1½ cups/400g tomato puree
½ tsp chilli powder
4 cups/1l water
1½ tsp salt

YOGHURT SAUCE
4 cups/1kg yoghurt
1 tbsp tahini
2 garlic cloves, crushed

1 medium pita bread, cut into squares and toasted

1. To make the meatballs mix the spices and chopped onions together. Add the meat and combine together. Sprinkle parsley over the meat and mix together. Shape into small meatballs, around 1½ centimetres in diameter. Heat the oil in a large frying pan. Carefully add the meatballs and fry until browned and well done.

2. Make the tomato sauce by sautéing the onions in the oil in a large pan (big enough to fit the meatballs later) over a low heat until soft. Add the cinnamon sticks and bay leaf. Stir in the tomato purée and water and bring to the boil. Reduce the heat and cook for 15 minutes.

3. To make the yoghurt sauce whisk the tahini and garlic together with ½ cup/125ml of the yoghurt until well blended. Add the rest of the yoghurt and continue mixing with the whisk.

4. Add the meatballs to the tomato sauce and cook for a further 10 minutes.

4. This is served on individual plates. Each person places the toasted bread first, then some meatballs with sauce and tops it with some yoghurt sauce. The quantities depend on personal preferences.

NOTES
You can substitute beef for lamb.

DIFFICULTY: ★

•KIBBEH   •PASTRIES   •STEWS   •SWEETS   •TABBOULEH   •VEGAN   •VEGETARIAN   •WHEAT FREE   •WILD EDIBLE PLANTS

ALL SEASON **APETIZERS, SIDE DISHES**
SERVES: 6

قريصه بالطحينه
KARISSA BIL TAHINI
KARISSA IN TAHINI SAUCE

1⅓ cups/300g burghul
   (bulgur wheat)
2 cups/500ml water
2½ cups/300g plain flour
⅛ tsp sumac
¼ tsp salt
1 onion small, grated

TAHINI SAUCE
1 cup/260g tahini
1 cup/250ml lemon juice
¼ tsp orange blossom water
1½ tsp salt

1. Place the burghul in a bowl. Add enough water to cover burghul by 1cm. Soak for 40 minutes.

2. Add the onion to the burghul and mix well. Add the flour, sumac and salt. Knead until homogeneous. It should have the consistency of a dough that you can make into balls.

3. Have a small bowl of cold water handy to dip your fingers in when the dough gets sticky. Shape the Karissa dough into 2cm discs. Drop the discs into a large pan of boiling water and cook for 30 minutes over a medium heat. Drain and place on a serving plate.

4. To make the tahini sauce mix all the ingredients together with a whisk

5. Pour the tahini sauce over the Karissa.

NOTES
This a dish that is traditionally served on Good Friday. Use Bou Sfeir juice (the juice of bitter or Seville oranges) if in season instead of the lemon juice.

DIFFICULTY: ★★
•KIBBEH   •PASTRIES   •STEWS   •SWEETS   •TABBOULEH   •VEGAN   •VEGETARIAN   •WHEAT FREE   •WILD EDIBLE PLANTS

ALL SEASON DESSERTS

MAKES: 4 DOZEN

معمول بالرّاحه
MAAMOUL BIL RAHA
LOKOUM MAAMOUL

6 cups/1kg semolina, coarse
1 cup/250g butter
⅓ cup/80ml milk
1 cup/200g sugar
½ cup/120ml orange blossom water
¼ tsp mastica grains (mastic gum), ground
½ cup/120ml rose water
loukoum, quantity as needed
icing sugar, optional

1. To make the dough mix the semolina, butter, milk, sugar, mastic powder, ¼ cup/60ml of the orange blossom water and ¼ cup/60ml of the rose water and knead until well combined. Cover and refrigerate overnight. Remove from the refrigerator a couple of hours before shaping into balls. When at room temperature add the remaining orange blossom and rose water and knead again until the consistency is of a workable dough.

2. Preheat the oven to 180°C/350°F/gas mark 4

3. Making the Maamoul: Cut the loukoum into 1cm cubes (approximately). Form into 2cm diameter balls. Press to form a hollow. Place a piece of loukoum in the centre and carefully close to cover all of the loukoum piece. Shape into a ball with a flat side (see photo). Place the balls on a tray with a 2cm space between the pieces.

4. Bake for 20 minutes or until slightly golden. Wait until fully cooled before removing from the tray.

5. Option If you prefer a sweeter version, sprinkle with icing sugar as soon as you take them out of the oven.

DIFFICULTY: ★★★

•KIBBEH   •PASTRIES   •STEWS   •SWEETS   •TABBOULEH   •VEGAN   •VEGETARIAN   •WHEAT FREE   •WILD EDIBLE PLANTS

THE NORTH
DOUMA

SAFAA SARKIS SHALHOUB

The bubbly Safaa Sarkis loves people and food and so being a guesthouse owner comes naturally to her. Her pride in Douma's culinary heritage is, however, offset by the fear that many of its cooking traditions may eventually be forgotten. "Most of our children do not have the time or inclination to prepare the traditional and sometimes time-consuming specialties," she explains. Still, today she is preparing Maacroon Bi Toum. Yes, with garlic. Because even though in most of Lebanon, *maacroon* are a sweet, in Douma they are savoury, similar to Italian gnocchi.

Her brother George is a ranger at the Tannourine Cedar Reserve as well as a guest house owner and guide on the Lebanon Mountain Trail. Safaa would cook whenever her help was needed and she took the opportunity to participate in training sessions offered by Atayeb (see Kfardebiane p86). "I always got ten out of ten!" she says proudly. "Everybody agreed my dishes were the tastiest."

Sitting in Safaa's warm kitchen, I notice an old stone inscription over a doorway. It reads "1914". I ask if that is the date when the house was built but I'm told it marks the date of one of the additions to the house. Safaa's husband, Joseph, tells me that his great, great grandfather built the original family home with his own hands in 1804. His family has lived in Douma for over 300 years.

Following nature's cues, Safaa is busy year-round, tending the family garden and orchards, harvesting and making her *mouneh*. In her sizeable pantry, I notice a large variety of pumpkins and squashes. Each one has a specific use: one is for a special butternut squash kibbeh typically prepared during lent, appropriately called Kibbet El Raheb or Monk's Kibbeh, another is for marmalade, and others each have their own specific destiny.

FALL, WINTER MAIN DISHES

SERVES: 10

KIBBET EL RAHEB
MONK'S KIBBEH

SOUP
1 cup/200g dried brown lentils, washed
1 cup/250ml olive oil
3 onions, chopped
1 bunch Swiss chard, stalks and leaves chopped

PUMPKIN KIBBEH BALLS
1 kg butternut squash
2 onions, quartered
¼ cup/5g fresh mint leaves
¼ cup/5g fresh marjoram leaves
¼ cup/5g fresh lemon balm
¼ cup/5g fresh basil leaves
½ tbsp seven spices
1 cup/225g brown burghul (bulgur wheat), fine
1 cup/120g plain flour
2 lemons, freshly squeezed
6 garlic cloves, crushed
1 tbsp sumac
1 ½ tsp salt

1. To make the soup boil the lentils in a large pan of water for 30 to 45 minutes until soft and drain. Set aside. Chop 3 of the onions. In a medium sized pan, sauté the 3 onions in the oil until golden. Add the lentils, Swiss chard and 8 cups/2l water. Cook until the lentils are well done

2. Preheat the oven to 180°C/350°F/gas mark 4. To make the kibbeh balls cut the squash lengthwise and spoon out the seeds and fibres. Place both halves face down on a baking tray. Cover with foil and bake in the oven until tender enough to scoop out the flesh. Scoop out the flesh and place in a sieve to remove any excess liquid. Place all the herbs, the remaining 2 onions and the seven spices in a food processor and blend until all the herbs are finely chopped. Place the unwashed burghul in a large bowl and add the pulp of the squash. Mix with a spoon and leave to rest for 15 minutes. Knead together and add the herb mixture. Add flour and continue kneading until the dough is firm. If needed add more flour until you have a malleable dough. Shape into 2cm balls and place all the balls on a floured tray. When all the balls have been added to the tray shake the tray horizontally until all the balls are lightly coated.

3. Bring lentil soup to the boil. Drop the kibbeh balls into the soup and cook for 10 minutes while stirring gently. Add the lemon juice, garlic, salt and sumac. Remove from the heat and serve.

DIFFICULTY: ★★★

•KIBBEH   •PASTRIES   •STEWS   •SWEETS   •TABBOULEH   •VEGAN   •VEGETARIAN   •WHEAT FREE   •WILD EDIBLE PLANTS

ALL SEASON MAIN DISHES

SERVES: 10

معكرون بالثوم
MAACROON BI TOUM
GNOCCHIS IN GARLIC SAUCE

DOUGH
1 cup/120g wholemeal flour
1 cup/120g white flour
½ tsp salt

GARLIC PUREE
5 garlic cloves, peeled
1½ tsp freshly squeezed lemon juice
1⅛ cups/280ml olive oil

1. To make the dough mix both types of flour and the salt. Gradually add some water and knead until the dough is moderately firm but not sticky. Knead for at least 10 minutes.

2. For the garlic purée place the garlic and salt in a food processor and chop at high speed. Keep the machine running and very slowly drizzle in the olive oil. The mixture will begin to form a paste with the consistency of mayonnaise. Drizzle the lemon juice slowly into the processor after the paste has formed, while the food processor is at high speed.

3. On a generously floured surface, flatten out the ball of dough using the palms of hands until evenly flat and about 1cm thick. Cut into 1cm wide strips. Cut each strip into 1cm pieces. Take a piece of dough and press and roll against the grain of a straw basket or sieve to form the shape of a gnocchi, as shown in the photos opposite. Place all of the dough pieces (maacroons) on a generously floured tray and shake the tray horizontally so all pieces of dough are well coated with flour.

4. Bring 10 cups/2½l of water to the boil with ¼ cup oil and 1 tbsp salt.

5. Gently drop the maacroon (dough) pieces one serving spoon at a time into the water. Cook for a minimum of 30 minutes. The maacroons should be well done – not al dente. The water will thicken to a creamy consistency. Gently fold in the garlic puree. Serve immediately while still hot.

DIFFICULTY: ★★★

•KIBBEH •PASTRIES •STEWS •SWEETS •TABBOULEH •VEGAN •VEGETARIAN •WHEAT FREE •WILD EDIBLE PLANTS

ALL SEASON **APPETIZERS**
SERVES: 8

مجدّره بالبرغل
MOUJADDARA BIL BURGHUL
BURGHUL LENTIL PILAF

1½ cups pink beans, (or borlotti beans) soaked overnight
3 cups/750ml water
1½ onions, chopped
¾ cups/170g burghul (bulgur wheat)
½ cup/125ml olive oil
1 tsp salt

1. Boil the beans in a pan of water until soft. Drain and return the beans to the pan.

2. In a separate pan sauté the onions in the oil until golden. Add to the beans. Add the burghul and cook for a further 10 minutes.

3. Serve with fattoush (or a seasonal salad), fries and pickles.

DIFFICULTY: ★★

•KIBBEH   •PASTRIES   •STEWS   •SWEETS   •TABBOULEH   •VEGAN   •VEGETARIAN   •WHEAT FREE   •WILD EDIBLE PLANTS

FALL DESSERTS

SERVES: 12

كباكيب سفرجل
KABAKEEB SAFARJAL
QUINCE BALLS

1kg quince
1kg sugar
200g blanched almond halves

1. Peel and cut the quinces into 8 slices and cut out the core. In a food processor, shred the quince slices on the large setting. Reweigh the shredded quinces to make sure that the weight is 1kg.

2. In a plastic bowl, mix the shredded quinces with the sugar. Cover and refrigerate overnight or for a minimum of 7 hours.

3. Place the quince and sugar in a pan and cook over a low heat, stirring frequently for about 2 hours. Make sure that all excess liquid has evaporated. To test whether it is ready take a spoonful of the mixture and let it cool until warm. If it can be shaped into a ball it is done. Otherwise continue cooking.

4. Pour a cup/200g of sugar onto a plate. Have a small bowl of water ready for dipping fingers. Allow the quince mixture to cool until warm, approximately 50°C/120°F. Shape into 2cm balls, occasionally dipping fingers into the water when palms get too sticky. Press an almond onto the centre of each ball and flatten into the shape of a doughnut. Gently press both sides onto the plate of sugar.

DIFFICULTY: ★

•KIBBEH •PASTRIES •STEWS •SWEETS •TABBOULEH •VEGAN •VEGETARIAN •WHEAT FREE •WILD EDIBLE PLANTS

THE NORTH
KFARDEBIANE

SAMIRA ZGHEIB

The humble two-storey white house has a sign above the black metal door: Atayeb (delicious food). We open the door and enter a room full of boxes, crates and sacks. Samira welcomes us with a generous, beaming smile.

We are somewhat taken aback when we enter the next room: it is immaculate and full of modern commercial food preparation equipment, manned by the adorable ladies of the co-operative who infuse these large stainless-steel cauldrons with their secret potion of love, generosity and pride.

When she graduated from high school in Kfardebiane, the normal thing would have been for Samira to become a schoolteacher – pretty much the only career option for a young woman of her background. But her persistent desire for self-improvement, intelligence, passion and intuitive entrepreneurship qualities propelled her to a different future.

The first opportunity she seized was a handcrafts training program at the convent of Deir El Saleeb. Then, when she had a chance to work with the Beirut YMCA, she used her skills to become an instructor. She would bring homemade fruit rolls and sweets from Kfardebiane to share with her colleagues. All agreed that they were not only delicious, but they were also healthy and different.

In time, however, Samira noticed that demand for the handcrafts they were making had declined sharply. She came up with the idea of making a bold and dramatic shift, moving operations to create locally sourced foods and preserves or *mouneh*, following the traditional home recipes. The YMCA agreed and she initiated Atayeb, the first pilot cooperative in Kfardebiane. Its success resulted in a network of 42 similar cooperatives, known as COOPs, all over the country.

Samira sought and acquired all the needed certifications and licenses for a food-related business. She also applied for and attained grants from several organizations supportive of rural development initiatives such as USAID, YMCA, UNDP and ICU. Through the course of this momentous journey she received countless certificates and awards of excellence, both locally and internationally.

Atayeb continues to grow and evolve in step with current food trends and is one of the few COOPs that maintains an export license. In addition to managing Atayeb, Samira conducts regular workshops and trainings for the other 42 COOPs in Lebanon that have followed the Atayeb model. She typically starts her workshops by saying, "I'm not here to teach you. I am here to answer your questions."

SUMMER **SIDE DISHES**

SERVES: 6

شمندر بالطحينه
SHAMANDAR BIL TAHINI
BEETROOT SALAD WITH TAHINI SAUCE

1kg beetroot, boiled and peeled
1 cup/270g tahini
2 cups/500ml freshly squeezed lemon juice
2 garlic cloves
2 tbsp olive oil
pinch sea salt
½ cup/15g fresh parsley, chopped

1. Cut the beetroot into medium-sized cubes and place in a salad bowl.

2. To make the taratour (tahini sauce) put the lemon juice in a small bowl. Crush the garlic with a pinch of salt and add to the lemon juice. Stir the tahini into the lemon juice and garlic until smooth and creamy. Adjust salt to taste.

3. Add the taratour to the beetroot and mix. Drizzle with the olive oil and sprinkle with the parsley. Serve with flat bread on the side.

DIFFICULTY: ★

•KIBBEH •PASTRIES •STEWS •SWEETS •TABBOULEH **•VEGAN** **•VEGETARIAN** **•WHEAT FREE** •WILD EDIBLE PLANTS

SUMMER **APPETIZERS, SIDE DISHES**

SERVES: 6

مدفونه

MADFOUNEH

GREEN BEANS WITH
TOMATOES AND RICE

1kg green beans

½kg onions

½kg tomatoes

1 cup/200g Italian rice (eg. Arborio)

2 tbsp olive oil

1 head of garlic

1 tsp salt

1 cup/250ml water

1. Wash the green beans. Snap or chop off the stem ends. Snap or chop into two or three pieces depending on the length of the beans.

2. Sauté the onions in the oil in a pan over a medium heat until lightly golden. Add the garlic and cook for another couple of minutes. Add the green beans to the pan, lower the heat and cook until softened but not fully cooked. Dice the tomatoes, add to the pan and cook until the tomatoes are soft and have formed a sauce – about ten minutes.

3. In a separate pan, bring the water to the boil and add the rice. Reduce the heat and cook covered for 15 minutes until the rice is done.

4. Serve the rice and vegetables together.

DIFFICULTY: ★

•KIBBEH   •PASTRIES   •STEWS   •SWEETS   •TABBOULEH   •VEGAN   •VEGETARIAN   •WHEAT FREE   •WILD EDIBLE PLANTS

ALL SEASON **DESSERTS**
MAKES: 18

صفوف بدبس التفّاح

SFOUF BI DEBS
APPLE MOLASSES CAKES

5 cups/600g flour
2½ cups/850g apple molasses
1 cup/250ml olive oil
½ cup/70g sesame seeds

1. Preheat the oven to 180°C/350°F/gas mark 4. Mix all the ingredients together in a large mixing bowl. Pour the mixture into a square cake tin. Sprinkle the sesame seeds evenly over the top. Place on the middle rack of the oven. Lower the heat to 120°C/250°F/gas mark ½. Bake for 20 minutes.

2. Cool on a wire rack. Cut into medium sized diamond-shaped pieces and serve the small diamond-shaped cakes on a plate.

DIFFICULTY: ★★

•KIBBEH   •PASTRIES   •STEWS   •SWEETS   •TABBOULEH   •VEGAN   •VEGETARIAN   •WHEAT FREE   •WILD EDIBLE PLANTS

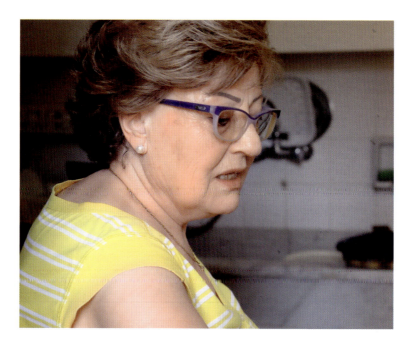

THE NORTH
MINIARA

ROSE EL-MURR

LA VIE EN ROSE

Rose's house, a quaint, three-story building on the top of the hill in Miniara, is light pink with pale pink shutters. Rose greets us excitedly, welcomes us into her home and insists that we sit with her for a cup of coffee before we start cooking. Houses are a reflection of their owners and this is certainly true of this house. Rose's china, color scheme and accessories all have her touch. She points out some beautiful pieces of lace and china that are from her bridal trousseau.

It is light and airy in her kitchen. Unlike most of the ladies I have met on my visits for this book, her daughter has written down all her recipes. "We all love to eat and cook," she says. "We treasure our traditional dishes." The Mtabbleh she will be making today is a peasant meal that they have been making in her area for generations. After a long hot day in the fields, farmers would have this simple, two-ingredient dish because it is filling, nutritious and cooling.

At first, I thought that she was wearing a training suit for comfort. Actually, this energetic great grandmother has a very busy life. She tells me she was up at 5:30 this morning. She had already prepared all the food for our visit and done her "rounds" on foot before we arrived at 9:30. Rose started an initiative in Miniara with a group of ladies through her church, preparing meals for the elderly and delivering them to their homes. She makes a point of checking on them every morning to say hello and see if they are ok. Rose believes that no one should ever want for food or the kindness of a smile.

ALL SEASON **APPETIZERS**
MAKES: 16

فطاير بالقريشه
FATAYER AREESHEH
MILK CURD TURNOVERS

DOUGH

8⅓ cups /1 kg flour
¾ cup/180ml water
¼ tsp salt
2 tbsp milk powder
½ cup sunflower oil
½ tsp dried yeast
¼ tsp granulated sugar

AREESHEH

1 tbsp salt
3 cups/750ml water
4½ cups/3 kg yoghurt

FILLING

1 tsp butter
1 onion, chopped
1 tsp dried mint
½ tsp chillli powder

1. Mix all the dough ingredients together in a large bowl and knead. The dough should be firm and not sticky. Leave the dough to rest covered for 30 minutes

2. Put all the areesheh ingredients in a blender and liquefy. Pour into a large pan and heat over a low heat until the mixture curdles. Strain in a cheesecloth overnight. In the morning squeeze out any excess liquid and transfer to a large bowl.

3. For the filling heat the butter in the microwave for 10 seconds and add to a bowl with the onions. Mix together so the onions are covered and leave to cool. Add the buttery onions, mint and chilli to the areesheh and mix well.

4. Making the pastries:
Flour a work surface and roll out the dough on it. Cut out circles using a pastry cutter of 9cm diameter.
Spoon a tablespoon of filling onto each dough circle.
Fold over each circle to form a half-moon and close by pressing firmly around the edge.

5. To cook
Option 1: Deep fry and strain on paper towels on a plate.
Option 2: Preheat the oven to 180°C/350°F/gas mark 4. Coat a baking tray with oil, brush the pastries with oil and bake until golden brown.

DIFFICULTY: ★★

•KIBBEH •PASTRIES •STEWS •SWEETS •TABBOULEH •VEGAN •VEGETARIAN •WHEAT FREE •WILD EDIBLE PLANTS

ALL SEASON **APPETIZERS**

SERVES: 6

متبله

MTABBLEH

WHOLE WHEAT
AND YOGHURT

1 cup/200g whole wheat grains, soaked overnight in water

4½ cups/1kg yoghurt

½ teaspoon salt

1. Drain the wheat in a colander and put in a large pan. Pour water over the wheat so that the water level is around 5 centimeters above it. Bring to the boil. Lower the heat and cook for one hour. The grains of wheat should be done but not too soft. Leave to cool to room temperature.

2. Whip the yoghurt with a whisk in a bowl. Add to the wheat in the pan. Cook for 15 minutes. This can be eaten at room temperature or chilled. Serve in cups or glasses.

NOTES

Yoghurt can either be cow's or goat's yoghurt. Mtabbleh is usually eaten as a snack in the afternoon or after dinner. Served chilled in the summer months.

DIFFICULTY: ★

•KIBBEH   •PASTRIES   •STEWS   •SWEETS   •TABBOULEH   •VEGAN   •VEGETARIAN   •WHEAT FREE   •WILD EDIBLE PLANTS

ALL SEASON **MAIN DISHES**
SERVES: 2

سمكة حرّه منياريه
SAMKEH HARRA MINIARIYYEH
MINIARA SPICY BAKED FISH

1 whole grouper, or fish of your choice, gutted and descaled

FILLING
1 tbsp fresh coriander
½ tsp chilli powder
4 garlic cloves, crushed
½ tsp salt
2 cups/200 g walnuts, coarsely chopped
3 tbsp fresh cilantro, chopped
1 tsp fish spices of your choice
2 tbsp olive oil

SAUCE
2 lemons, squeezed
½ cup/125ml water
¼ cup olive oil

DIFFICULTY: ★★

1. Wash the fish. Rinse with a mixture of vinegar and water. Pat dry.

2. Mix all the filling ingredients together in a large bowl.

3. Stuff the belly cavity of the fish with the filling. Reserve any leftover filling. Sew the cavity together with a needle and thread. Score the fish once on both sides. Rub with salt and spices. Set aside for 15 minutes. Heat 2tbsp oil in a large frying pan. Brown the fish for 5min on each side. Mix water, salt, oil and lemon juice. Add to pan with remaining filling. Sauté fish for 3 minutes on each side.

NOTES
Fish size should be enough to serve 2.

•KIBBEH   •PASTRIES   •STEWS   •SWEETS   •TABBOULEH   •VEGAN   •VEGETARIAN   •**WHEAT FREE**   •WILD EDIBLE PLANTS

WEST BEQAA

WEST BEQAA
AIN ZEBDEH

NOHA ABI RACHED

Just as peoples' homes are often a reflection of who they are, so too can villages be a reflection of their villagers. Ain Zebdeh lies perched on a green hill overlooking Lake Qaraoun, its immaculately maintained homes and gardens noticeable even from a distance. It is a manifestation of the spirit of community and caring that its residents possess. Noha Abi Rached's humble home is on the town square. She takes great pride that her father, a farmer, built it with his own hands, hauling the massive supporting ceiling beams all the way from the Litani river with the help of some young friends from the village. Noha's front door is never locked, the invitation "Mayylu" if not always voiced is always implied as is evidenced by the steady stream of visitors and the pot of coffee that is always on the stove or *sobia*.

FALL **APPETIZERS, SIDE DISHES**

SERVES: 6

بطاطا حمرة بالطرطور
BATATA HAMRA BIL TARATOUR
RED POTATOES IN TAHINI SAUCE

1kg red potatoes

FOR THE TARATOUR
1 cup/270g tahini
½ cup/120ml lemon Juice
1 garlic clove, crushed
¼ cup/60ml olive oil

1. Boil the potatoes with skin on until fully cooked, but do not allow to become soft.

2. To make the taratour, mix the tahini with the lemon juice and garlic in a small bowl. If necessary, add a little water until it has a creamy consistency.

3. Pour the taratour sauce over the potatoes and mix gently until all the potatoes are coated. Serve at room temperature.

NOTES
These red potatoes are only grown in Ain Zebdeh and inside they are a lovely rose color. If not available they can be substituted with any salad potato.

DIFFICULTY:

•KIBBEH   •PASTRIES   •STEWS   •SWEETS   •TABBOULEH   **•VEGAN**   •VEGETARIAN   •WHEAT FREE   •WILD EDIBLE PLANTS

ALL SEASON **APPETIZERS**

MAKES: 24

كبة بطاطا باللبنه و القورما

KIBBET BATATA BIL QAWARMA
POTATO KIBBEH STUFFED WITH LABNEH AND QAWARMA

2kg potatoes, boiled with the skins on
3 cups/675g burghul (bulgur wheat)
1 large onion, grated
2 tbsp salt
1 tsp seven spices

FOR THE STUFFING
½kg qawarma
1kg labneh (see page 196)

1. Peel the boiled potatoes and mash. Combine the potatoes together with the burghul and seven spices in a mixing bowl until a dough is formed. The colour should be light (see photo). Add the grated onion and mix well. Make a depression in the dough in the shape of a cross. Leave to cool.

2. To make the stuffing, mix the labneh and qawarma together.

3. Stuffing the kibbehs:
1. Form the potato and burghul dough into balls around 4cm in diameter.
2. Insert a finger into the middle of the ball. While rotating the dough press against the sides of dough to produce a hollow oval.
3. Spoon the stuffing into the hollow until it is filled.
4. Squeeze together the sides of the opening to close. Shape into a patty, dipping fingers into a bowl of water to smooth the surface
5. Place patties in a pan or roasting dish over the hob. As each side of the patties is seared, turn over carefully until all sides are done (slightly charred).

NOTES
Qawarma may be substituted with browned minced beef.

DIFFICULTY: ★★★

•**KIBBEH** •PASTRIES •STEWS •SWEETS •TABBOULEH •VEGAN •VEGETARIAN •WHEAT FREE •WILD EDIBLE PLANTS

A CELEBRATION OF TOGETHERNESS

Vera Bou Mounsef

Lebanon's civil war ended in 1990, but the conflict left many divisions in Lebanon's social fabric, as the small town of Ain Zebdeh knows all too well. But Vera Bou Mounsef, a feisty young journalist, resolved to find a way to restore the community spirit of her town.

The Feast of the Cross, or *Eid El Saleeb,* has always been a special event in Ain Zebdeh. The women of the town are proud of their reputation for making the best potato kibbeh with labneh and qawarma. And so in 1992 Vera, combining faith and pride in their heritage, the two values that all the villagers shared no matter their political affiliations, gave the women a challenge: to make over 100 pieces of Ain Zebdeh's famous kibbeh and sell them during the feast to raise money for the church.

The ladies of Ain Zebdeh rose to the challenge and it was a success. Now, the whole town - women, men, children, teenagers – all take part. Some even come back from abroad just for the event. Everyone pitches in, either in the logistics, the actual work, financially or all of the above and for two days the town is transformed into one big bustling communal kitchen. The number of kibbeh made for the festival has grown and grown.

In August 2018, the parish priest of Ain Zebdeh, Father Joseph, distributes the meat for the qawarma to the best cooks in town. On the eve of the feast, 300 kilograms of potatoes, donated by a local farmer, are delivered to the Church basement, where an army of cleaners scrub and wash them. At 4am, Father Joseph and a group of young men crank up the fires and boil the potatoes. At 7am the workforce shows up for peeling and mashing. Then everyone rests ahead of the marathon kibbeh-making session that begins at noon.

The big hall of the church buzzes with the happy chatter of over 40 women, with a troupe of little "elves" in tow filling in for the support tasks. The atmosphere is full of merriment, adrenaline and a seamless harmony. They are all determined to beat last year's record. At around 4pm, the designated "counter", a teenage boy, who has been taking his responsibilities very seriously, announces that 4,350 pieces of kibbeh have been made. The record has been broken.

In the evening, after the mass of *Eid El Saleeb* in the beautiful new church, the town is one big party, with live music, lights, cooking and a lot of spontaneous dancing. People come from far and wide to join in the festivities.

Food has always brought people together. In Ain Zebdeh they do it in a big way. The sense of unity and belonging in this town is palpable as Vera Bou Mounsef's vision of over 25 years ago blossomed into something beyond even her expectations.

ALL SEASON **MAIN DISHES**
SERVES: 8

ZINKOL

3 cups/675g burghul (bulgur wheat)
½ kg pumpkin, peeled and cut into cubes
⅛ tsp seven spices
3 tsp salt
¼ cup/30g plain flour, as needed
1 cup/175g chickpeas, soaked in water overnight
4 medium onions, finely chopped
1 cup/250ml sunflower oil
1½ garlic heads, peeled into cloves and chopped fine
½ cup/125ml apple vinegar
¼ cup/80g debs hosrom (hosrom molasses)
1 tbsp dried mint

1. To make the zinkol dough, boil the pumpkin in a large pan of water until soft. Drain well and transfer to a large mixing bowl. Add the burghol and flour and mix together. Leave to rest for 15 minutes. Test if firm enough to be malleable. If still sticky and soft add a little more flour.

2. Shape the zinkol dough into marble size balls and place on a tray.

3. Cook the chickpeas in a large pan of boiling water until soft – usually about half an hour. Gently drop the zinkol balls into the same pan. Add salt, cover and cook for 5-10 min or until zinkol balls float to the top.

4. In a frying pan gently fry the onions until golden brown. Add to the chickpeas and zinkol balls. Stir in the garlic, mint, vinegar and hosrom.

NOTES
Debs hosrum can be substituted with ¼ cup/60ml of balsamic vinegar. Soaked and boiled chickpeas can be substituted by two tins of chickpeas.

DIFFICULTY: ★★★

•KIBBEH   •PASTRIES   •STEWS   •SWEETS   •TABBOULEH   •VEGAN   •VEGETARIAN   •WHEAT FREE   •WILD EDIBLE PLANTS

FALL, WINTER SIDE DISHES

SERVES: 8

منسوفة يقطين

MANSOUFIT LAKTEEN
PUMPKIN MANSOUF

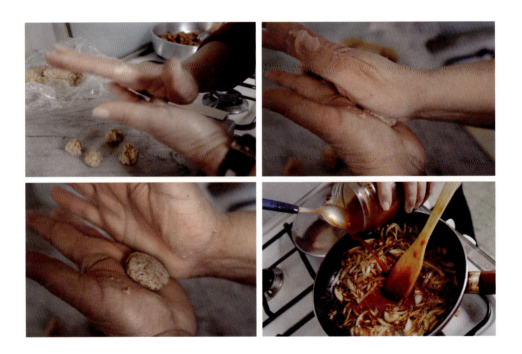

Zinkol dough (see page 30)
8 cups/2l water
1 tbsp salt
14 onions, sliced
1 cup/250ml olive oil
½ cup/125ml sharab hosrom

1. Shape the zinkol dough into 2cm patties. Bring the water and salt to the boil in a large pan. Drop the patties into the water. Cover and cook for 5 minutes. Drain through a colander and place the patties on a shallow platter.

2. In a large frying pan fry the onions in the oil over a medium heat until golden brown. Spoon out most of the oil and discard. Add the hosrom to the onions and stir well. Spoon the onions over the zinkol patties.

NOTES
Hosrum can be substituted with balsamic vinegar.

DIFFICULTY: ★★

•KIBBEH   •PASTRIES   •STEWS   •SWEETS   •TABBOULEH   •**VEGAN**   •**VEGETARIAN**   •WHEAT FREE   •WILD EDIBLE PLANTS

ALL SEASON **MAIN DISHES**

SERVES: 10

زنكل باللبن
ZINKOL BIL LABAN
ZINKOL WITH YOGHURT

2kg yoghurt

4 tbsp cornflour

10 garlic cloves, peeled and crushed

2 tbsp olive oil

1 portion zinkol dough (which serves 8) (see page 30)

2 tbsp dried mint

1. Fry the garlic in the oil over a low heat until slightly browned.

2. In a mixing bowl whisk the cornflour and yoghurt together until smooth. Put a pan on medium heat and add the yoghurt mix. Add the fried garlic and bring to the boil. Drop the zinkol balls into the yoghurt and then lower the heat. Sprinkle the dried mint into the mix and cook, stirring gently for 8 minutes.

3. Serve in a tureen or deep bowl.

NOTES
Hosrum can be substituted with balsamic vinegar.

DIFFICULTY: ★★★

•KIBBEH   •PASTRIES   •STEWS   •SWEETS   •TABBOULEH   **•VEGAN**   **•VEGETARIAN**   •WHEAT FREE   •WILD EDIBLE PLANTS

ALL SEASON **MAIN DISHES**
SERVES: 4

مفرّكة البطاطا
MOUFARRAKET BATATA
POTATO AND MEAT STIR FRY

10 garlic cloves, chopped
100g minced beef
4 potatoes (large), cubed
1 tsp seven spices
1 tbsp chilli paste
1 cup/250ml sunflower oil
Salt

1. In a large frying pan fry the potatoes over a medium heat until slightly browned. Set aside.

2. In a deep pan, fry the onions and garlic over a medium heat until golden. Add the beef and cook until well browned and all liquid has evaporated. Add the fried potatoes (above) along with the spices and chilli paste and stir all together. Serve on a platter while still warm.

DIFFICULTY: ★

•KIBBEH •PASTRIES •STEWS •SWEETS •TABBOULEH •VEGAN •VEGETARIAN •WHEAT FREE •WILD EDIBLE PLANTS

WEST BEQAA
AITANIT

LABIBEH AL RASSY

Labibeh's quaint little garden in the entrance to her house is full of spring flowers and aromatic herbs. It is the week before Palm Sunday and the time when the ladies in Aitanit traditionally start preparing Kaak El Shaanineh. These kaak are prepared in many other villages, but in Aitanit they make them with a special ingredient: marjoram.

Labibeh takes us to her sunny front porch that has a magnificent view of Lake Qaraoun, the stillness reflecting in her eyes. She prefers to work there because it is a bright happy place.

Labibeh dries and preserves all of her spices and herbs (from her garden, of course) and there are bunches of herbs hanging everywhere. Their combined fragrance creates a unique bouquet that imbues the whole house. That day, she apologises for appearing a bit rushed, but sadly, she has to go to a friend's funeral. As in most of these small communities, the whole village will be attending. Aitanit is a very close-knit community.

Just as we are leaving, Labibeh's husband, Jamil, comes home. She gives his sweater a gentle tug and asks him why he is wearing it inside out. "This is the trend now Labibeh. I always wear the trendiest clothes for you," he says with a playful wink. He expresses his regret that he missed having coffee with us but we promise him to spend time with them again soon.

ALL SEASON **DESSERTS**

MAKES: 48

كعك الشعنينه
KAAK EL SHAANINEH
PALM SUNDAY COOKIES

2 cups/680g grape molasses
2 cups/500ml milk
8 cups/1kg plain flour
1 cup/160g semolina flour
1 tbsp dried yeast
¼ cup/60ml sunflower oil
1 cup/227g butter, melted
1 tbsp baking powder
1 tbsp dried marjoram

1. To make the dough put the flour in a large bowl. Remove one cup/125g of the flour from the bowl and set aside. Add the semolina flour and marjoram and mix together. Sprinkle the yeast over the dry ingredients. Mix the grape molasses with the milk in a separate bowl. Add to the dry ingredients and knead together. Place in a bowl, cover and keep in a warm place for a minimum of 6 hours.

2. Preheat the oven to 180°C/350°F/gas mark4 15 minutes before baking the cookies.

3. Lightly grease two baking trays. Shape the dough into 5cm sized balls. Press the dough balls into mould and cast out onto trays, or, if no moulds available, shape into cookies. Bake for 10 minutes or until golden brown.

NOTES
Use the largest size kaak mould – usually 9cm diameter.

DIFFICULTY: ★★★

•KIBBEH   •PASTRIES   •STEWS   •**SWEETS**   •TABBOULEH   •VEGAN   •**VEGETARIAN**   •WHEAT FREE   •WILD EDIBLE PLANTS

WEST BEQAA
KHERBET QANAFAR

LINA HADDAD

Lina is dismissive of the scar on her arm. "I broke my arm a few months ago," she explains. "I haven't regained all the strength in it yet. But it's ok. I can cook now. It's no big deal." Actually, it was. It meant the loss of several months of precious income, but Lina is a survivor and she has learned to adapt in a precarious economy.

Unlike many of the women I met on this culinary journey, Lina only recently taught herself cooking, after she lost her job teaching at Kherbet Qanafar's primary school. She had always cooked for her family, but now she needed to up her game to make the additional income needed to put her children through college.

"It happened quite by mistake," she tells me. "I had just lost my job and one of my neighbours needed help harvesting his mulberry trees. So, I thought that would be easy additional income. It was a bountiful harvest and he asked me if I knew how to make mulberry syrup. I almost said no. Then I thought how hard can it be to make mulberry syrup? I set out to find the best recipes and started experimenting. I discovered three things: that I wanted to make the best mulberry syrup, that I loved cooking and that I could make a living doing something I loved. I have been cooking for a living ever since." And yes, she is now known in all the surrounding villages for making the best mulberry syrup.

Like many women in the mountains, Lina also uses her *sobia* for cooking. This flat topped furnace, common in so many Lebanese homes, sits in the middle of the room to give heat in winter. As I sat stirring the pot of kishk, a type of mountain porridge, I noticed that it did not have the sharp smell that I am accustomed to, but instead rather smelt sweet. "My kishk is special," she smiles. "I get my burghul from a village in the Beqaa called Mansoura, where my supplier, a local farmer, plants his own wheat, which he harvests and dries himself. It is the best burghul for kishk. Then, I get my yoghurt from the monastery of Deir Ain El Jawzeh, where the goats graze only on oak trees. That's why it smells so sweet."

Seasonal foraging is part of a way of life, one that is in touch with the land and in tune with nature's cycles.

WINTER SIDE DISHES

SERVES: 6

بلغصون

BALGHASSOUN
ANCHUSA FRITTERS

300g balghassoun, washed
3 cups/750ml sunflower oil
6 eggs
2 tsp baking powder
3 tbsp plain flour
1 tsp black pepper powder
1 tsp salt
½ cup/125ml milk

1. In a large pan of boiling water blanch the balghassoun leaves, keeping them in the connected bunches. Strain well.

2. Heat the oil in a pan for deep frying.

3. In a large mixing bowl whisk the eggs together. Whisk the flour, baking powder, pepper, salt and milk into the eggs until a smooth batter is formed. Take each bunch of leaves and dip them into the batter.

4. Drop into the hot oil. When golden brown remove with a slotted spoon. Place some paper towels on plates and place the battered balghassoun on the towels to remove any excess oil. Serve while still hot.

NOTES
Balghassoun is a foraged plant that is found in winter. Some of the villages have been successful in cultivating it.

DIFFICULTY: ★

•KIBBEH   •PASTRIES   •STEWS   •SWEETS   •TABBOULEH   •VEGAN   •VEGETARIAN   •WHEAT FREE   •WILD EDIBLE PLANTS

WINTER **APPETIZER, SIDE DISHES**

SERVES: 10

دردر على حمّص
DARDAR A HOMMOS
SPANISH THISTLE WITH CHICKPEAS

1½kg dardar – unfortunately there is no substitute

4 large onions, sliced

1½ cups/375ml sunflower oil

4 cups/700g dried chickpeas, soaked overnight with 1 tsp of bicarbonate of soda

1 lemon, freshly squeezed

½ cup olive oil

2½ tsp salt

1. Pick out any undesirable leaves from the dardar. Place the dardar in a tub of water and leave to soak for a few minutes. Remove from the water and drain through a colander to remove the sand. Repeat until there is no more sand left at the bottom of the tub. Chop into medium strips about 2cm wide.

2. Drop the leaves into a large pan of boiling water and cook uncovered until tender. Remove the leaves from the water with a slotted spoon and place in a colander to drain, leaving to stand for at least an hour.

3. In a large pan fry the onions in the sunflower oil over a medium heat until golden brown. Boil the chickpeas in a large pan of water for 1½ hours until soft. Drain the chickpeas and transfer them to the pan with the onions. (If substituting tinned chick peas, use three tins, and there is no need to boil.) Lower the heat and stir gently. Stir in the dardar and lemon juice. Remove from the heat and add the olive oil and salt to taste. Serve on a shallow platter.

DIFFICULTY: ★

•KIBBEH   •PASTRIES   •STEWS   •SWEETS   •TABBOULEH   **•VEGAN**   **•VEGETARIAN**   **•WHEAT FREE**   **•WILD EDIBLE PLANTS**

SUMMER, FALL **APPETIZERS**

SERVES: 6

مينيّة برغل

MAINIYYET BULGUR
WILD JUTE MALLOW

½kg mainiyyeh
1½kg onions, sliced
1 garlic head, peeled and chopped
½ cup/120ml vegetable oil
juice of 1 lemon
3 tbsp olive oil
½ cup/75g whole almonds, blanched and peeled
½ cup burghul (bulgur wheat)
½ tbsp butter
2 tbsp vegetable oil

1. Wash the mainiyyieh leaves very well. Soak for 30 minutes and drain in a colander.

2. Lightly toast the almonds by frying them in the 2 tbsp of vegetable oil and ½ tbsp of butter.

3. In a medium pan, sauté the onions in ½ cup/120ml vegetable oil until soft. Add the chopped garlic and continue cooking over a medium heat until golden. Set aside half of the onions. Add all of the mainiyyeh leaves and cover the pan. When the leaves have wilted add the burghul and cook for another 10 minutes. Stir in the olive oil and lemon juice. Cook for 1 minute and remove from heat.

4. Serve on a shallow platter. Top with the almonds and the remaining onions.

DIFFICULTY: ★

•KIBBEH •PASTRIES •STEWS •SWEETS •Tabbouleh •VEGAN •VEGETARIAN •WHEAT FREE •WILD EDIBLE PLANTS

ALL SEASON APPETIZERS, SIDE DISHES

SERVES: 6

KIBBET JOZ
WALNUT KIBBEH

½ kg potatoes, boiled and peeled
1½ cups/340g burghul (bulgur wheat), fine
1 onion, coarsely grated
1 cup/100g walnuts, coarsely chopped in a food processor
1 tsp ground black pepper
1 tsp cinnamon powder
a pinch of grated nutmeg
1 tsp salt

1. Mash the boiled potatoes in the pan. Lina likes to do this manually with a potato masher, but you can use a hand blender. At the end, they should have a smooth, creamy consistency. Add the burghul to the hot mashed potatoes and mix well by hand.

2. Add the walnuts, onion, salt and spices to the mashed potatoes and mix well by hand.

3. Serve in a shallow platter. Decorate with fresh mint leaves and serve with green onions and olive oil.

NOTES
You can put the boiled potatoes in a food processor, but Lina prefers the manual method.

DIFFICULTY: ★★

•KIBBEH   •PASTRIES   •STEWS   •SWEETS   •TABBOULEH   •VEGAN   •VEGETARIAN   •WHEAT FREE   •WILD EDIBLE PLANTS

ALL SEASON **APPETIZERS**

MAKES: 12

كبة يقطين

LINA'S KIBBET YAKTEEN
PUMPKIN KIBBEH

FILLING
4 onions, sliced
½ cup/120ml sunflower oil
1½ cups/250g chickpeas, soaked overnight (or two tins)
1 tbsp bicarbonate of soda
2 cups/450g hommaida (sorrel) (can be substituted with Swiss chard)
1 cup/100g walnuts
2 tsp pomegranate molasses
salt, to taste
½ tsp ground black pepper

KIBBEH DOUGH
4 cups/900g burghul
1 cup/165g semolina flour
1 tsp ground black pepper
5 kg fresh pumpkin, peeled, cut and boiled
1 tsp kibbeh spices
1 tsp salt
½ nutmeg clove

1. Drain the soaked chickpeas in a colander. Sprinkle with bicarbonate of soda. Mix until coated evenly. Leave to stand for 7 minutes. Rinse well. Place in a pan of water and bring to the boil. Reduce heat to low. Partially cover. Cook until done, for around 15 minutes. Drain. If using tinned chickpeas, skip this stage.

2. Fry the onions in a large pan over a medium heat until golden. Add the chickpeas and sauté until any liquid has evaporated. Add the hommaida and walnuts. Mix well. Remove from the heat and add the pomegranate molasses, salt and pepper.

3. Kibbeh dough: Drain the boiled pumpkin well in a colander, squeezing out any excess liquid and reserve the cooking liquid. Put the burghul in a large bowl. Add the hot pumpkin to the burghul. Mix with a wooden spoon until well blended. Add the semolina flour, salt and all the spices. When not too hot, knead well by hand. Set aside to rest for 30 minutes. Take the kibbeh dough, roll into balls and fill with the filling.

4. Deep fry the kibbeh balls, place on paper towels to remove any excess oil. These can be oven baked rather than deep frying if you prefer. To do so, coat the kibbehs with oil and place on a greased oven tray, and bake for 30 minutes at 200°C/400°F/gas mark 6, checking at intervals.

DIFFICULTY: ★★★

•KIBBEH •PASTRIES •STEWS •SWEETS •TABBOULEH •VEGAN •VEGETARIAN •WHEAT FREE •WILD EDIBLE PLANTS

FILLING

KIBBET DOUGH

KIBBEH STEPS

FALL, WINTER **MAIN DISHES**

MAKES: 12

كبة يقطين بالكشك

KIBBET YAKTEEN BI KISHK
KISHK SOUP WITH PUMPKIN KEBBEH

FILLING
2 tbsp sunflower oil
1 onion, chopped
500g minced beef
2 tsp cinnamon powder
1 tsp salt

KIBBEH DOUGH
(see page 138)

KISHK SOUP
3 garlic cloves, chopped
¼ cup sunflower oil
1 cup/200g Egyptian rice (short grain rice)
1 cup/120g kishk

1. To make the filling fry the onions in a pan over a low heat until soft. Add the beef to the onions and cook until browned. Add cinnamon and salt to taste.

2. Make kibbeh dough and then make into kibbeh balls (see page 141, step 3). Fill with the onion and meat filling.

3. Soak the rice in a large bowl of water for 30 minutes. To make the kishk soup, lightly sauté the garlic with the oil in a large pan over a low heat. Drain the rice and add to the pan of sautéed garlic. Stir well for around 1 minute until the rice is coated in the oil. Add one cup/250ml of water and turn up the heat to a medium heat. When the rice is done – usually about ten minutes – gradually add the kishk until it is fully dissolved. Bring to the boil. Add the reserved pumpkin liquid (now at room temperature) until it has a creamy consistency. Gently drop the kibbeh balls into the kishk soup and cook on medium heat for approximately 5 minutes. Serve in soup bowls.

NOTES
There is no substitute for the ingredient kishk.

DIFFICULTY: ★★★★

•KIBBEH •PASTRIES •STEWS •SWEETS •TABBOULEH •VEGAN •VEGETARIAN •WHEAT FREE •WILD EDIBLE PLANTS

The happy, free-range goats of Deir Ain El Jawzweh

The monastery has a collaboration with Hassan Serhal, his brother Mohammad and their herd of 500 goats for the production of various goats' milk products, one of which is Lina Haddad's secret recipe in her yummy kishk.

Sun drying kishk on Lina's rooftop with the Anti-Lebanon mountains and the Beqaa Valley in the foreground.

ALL SEASON **DESSERTS**

MAKES: 3KG

كعك بحليب
KAAK BI HALEEB
EASTER COOKIES

4½ cups/590l milk
3¾ cups/750g white sugar
1½ cups/275ml sunflower oil
12 cups/1½kg plain flour
2 cups/165g semolina flour
½ tsp mahlab powder
1½ tsp baking powder
½ tsp dried yeast
½ tsp vanilla extract
½ clove nutmeg, freshly grated
1 tsp salt
¼ cup/60ml orange blossom water
1 cup/150g untoasted sesame seeds
¼ cup/50g granulated sugar

1. Pour the milk into a large non-stick pan and bring it to a gentle simmer. Lower the heat and add the sugar. Stir until the sugar is well dissolved. Add the oil and stir well. Then turn off heat.

2. To make the dough combine the plain flour, semolina, mahlab, baking powder, yeast, vanilla extract, nutmeg and salt in a large bowl. Add the milk mixture and stir well with a wooden spoon. Then mix by hand until thick and sticky. If it is too sticky add a bit more oil. Add the orange blossom water at the end. Mix and cover with cling film. Wrap in a blanket and place in a warm place. Leave to rise for 3 hours.

3. Preheat the oven to 150°C/300°F/gas mark 2. Grease two baking trays with sunflower oil and preheat the trays in the oven for 5 minutes.

4. Mix the sesame seeds with the sugar in a flat dish or tray. Roll the dough into 2cm diameter balls. Press the dough balls on to the sesame mixture. Press them, sesame side down, into the pattern of the mould (see photos 1 & 2). Flatten to 1cm thick rounds. Place sesame side up on trays.

5. Bake for 5-10 minutes, or until tops are lightly browned. Place on cooling racks.

NOTES
Typically made on Easter Sunday.

DIFFICULTY: ★★

•KIBBEH   •PASTRIES   •STEWS   •**SWEETS**   •TABBOULEH   •VEGAN   •**VEGETARIAN**   •WHEAT FREE   •WILD EDIBLE PLANTS

148

FALL, WINTER DESSERTS

MAKES: 10

زلابية يقطين

ZALABIET YAKTEEN
PUMPKIN FRITTERS

1kg pumpkin cubes, boiled
3 tbsp sugar
3 cups flour
½ tsp mahlab
½ tsp anis powder
1 tsp baking powder
1 tsp yeast
4 tbsp cornflour
3 tbsp vegetable oil

1. Strain pumpkin and save liquid for use in dough.

2. To make the batter mix all dry ingredients together well in a bowl. Add oil and pumpkin and mix further. Add some of the pumpkin liquid if needed to bring this to a soft and sticky texture (see photo). Cover the bowl and leave to rise in a warm place for 30 minutes.

3. Pour a generous amount of oil in a wok or deep pan and, once hot, drop 3 to 4 tablespoon size portions of the mix into hot oil, taking care to leave some space between them. Once the underside of the fritters has turned golden brown, turn over and cook until other side is also browned.

4. Place on serving dish and keep warm. Sprinkle with granulated sugar.

DIFFICULTY: ★

•KIBBEH   •PASTRIES   •STEWS   •SWEETS   •TABBOULEH   •VEGAN   •VEGETARIAN   •WHEAT FREE   •WILD EDIBLE PLANTS

WEST BEQAA
KHRAIYZAT

THERESE KHOURY

Walking through her vegetable garden, Thérèse Khoury gestures to the left-over ashes from the shisha pipes that are excellent nutrients for the fruit and vegetables, which, she points out with pride, are served at the restaurant she owns with her husband.

Winding through almond and apple orchards she leads us to an idyllic spot with tall trees and a bubbling brook. This is her favorite spot for foraging watercress, even if her knees are not what they used to be and she now must delegate the precarious task of foraging in cold streams to her husband and son.

"It is very important to know your water source when foraging for watercress because it absorbs pollutants in the water like a sponge. This spot has clean running water".

The simply-named "Abou Elias's Restaurant" sits nestled between tall willows and poplars. I marvel at how, from such a tiny kitchen, they are able to produce so much food. They work harmoniously and seamlessly. Every dish is served with a smile and a generosity of spirit.

Their guests today are a group from Beirut who have come on a field trip organized by the Food Heritage Foundation to learn about edible wild plants, one of Thérèse's specialities. They started off their day in the fields of the Beqaa and are ending it sampling Thérèse's special mezze in the shade of overhead straw mats. Their meal is accompanied by Abou Elias's traditional Lebanese improvisational poetry (or *zajal*), a goblet drum or *derbake* and the sound of the nearby gushing stream.

SPRING APPETIZERS, SIDE DISHES

SERVES: 8

دردر متبّل

DARDAR MTABBAL
DARDAR WITH LEMON AND GARLIC

2kg dardar
2 lemons, freshly squeezed
¼ cup/60ml olive oil
3 garlic cloves, crushed

1. Pick out any undesirable leaves from the dardar. Place the dardar in a tub of water and leave to soak for a few minutes. Remove from the water and drain through a colander to remove the sand. Repeat until there is no more sand left at the bottom of the tub. Chop coarsely.

2. Bring a large pan of salted water to the boil. Add the dardar and cook for 10 minutes or until the stems are soft. Drain and leave to cool until the dardar is cool enough to handle. Squeeze out any excess liquid.

3. In a bowl, mix in the remaining ingredients. Transfer to a serving dish. Serve at room temperature with bread of choice.

DIFFICULTY: ★

•KIBBEH •PASTRIES •STEWS •SWEETS •TABBOULEH •VEGAN •VEGETARIAN •WHEAT FREE •WILD EDIBLE PLANTS

SPRING **APPETIZERS, SIDE DISHES**

SERVES: 8

SAIFI

3 onions, chopped

2 tbsp olive oil

2 garlic cloves

salt, to taste

2kg saifi, cleaned and coarsely chopped

1 cup/175g dried chickpeas, soaked overnight and boiled for half an hour. If using tinned chickpeas, two tins, and no need to boil. Alternatively, use 1 cup/225g of burghul (bulgur wheat) together with ½ cup/125ml of boiling water

1. In a large pan sauté the onions in the olive oil over a medium heat until golden. Add the garlic and sauté for another 3 minutes.

2. Add the saifi to the pan and cook until wilted. Add the chickpeas, turn down to a low heat and continue cooking until the saifi is cooked through. Add salt to taste. Serve at room temperature.

DIFFICULTY: ★

•KIBBEH   •PASTRIES   •STEWS   •SWEETS   •TABBOULEH   •VEGAN   •VEGETARIAN   •WHEAT FREE   •WILD EDIBLE PLANTS

WEST BEQAA
SAGHBINE

JOUMANA CHEDID

Joumana Chedid is one of the cooks who host a Table d'Hôte on the West Beqaa Food Trail *(Darb El Karam)*. This initiative from the Food Heritage Foundation has opened up new economic opportunities in areas that have seen a significant migration of residents to Lebanon's towns and cities. Most of Saghbine's young generation live and work in cities, and although many come back home for the weekend, during the week the town is almost deserted.

"On Good Friday, every house in Saghbine serves Zinkol Bi Hamod," Joumana tells me. This generations-old tradition is a symbolic reference to Christ being given vinegar to drink instead of water before his crucifixion. Many villages do the same, but in Saghbine they add marjoram and substitute lemon juice for vinegar, serving the vinegar on the side.

Joumana's husband, Nabil, comes into the kitchen hovering over the steaming pots. He has that "when's-lunch?" look on his face, one that is a reflection of an outdoor life. Indeed, I had noticed many vintage farming and gardening tools displayed on the outside terrace and he tells me they were his father's and grandfather's - still in use to this day.

She tells him to be patient and so he goes back outside where he plays with his two small grandsons. "He'll just have to wait like the rest of us," she says with a wink.

SPRING, SUMMER **SIDE DISHES**

SERVES: 6

تبّوله بالقورما

TABBOULEH BIL QAWARMA
TABBOULEH WITH QAWARMA

1½ cups/360g qawarma

3 large bunches parsley, coarsely chopped

1 cup/25g fresh mint, chopped

1 small onion, chopped

½ tsp ground black pepper

⅛ tsp chilli flakes, optional

¼ cup/55g brown burghul (bulgur wheat), fine

½ cup/90g dried chickpeas, boiled and peeled

1 lemon, freshly squeezed

8 cabbage leaves

1. Heat the qawarma in a frying pan until all the fat has melted and is bubbling.

2. In a large bowl mix the chopped parsley and mint together. Add the chickpeas to the herbs along with the burghul and onions. Sprinkle the spices over the top of the onions and mix all the ingredients together. Pour over the lemon juice and gently mix.

3. Blanch the cabbage leaves quickly in a large pan of boiling water so the leaves are just slightly softened.

4. Just before serving, add the hot qawarma to the chickpeas, burghul and herbs and mix well. Serve while still hot in a large bowl.

NOTES

Must be served while the qawarma is still hot. How to eat: place a large spoonful of the tabbouleh onto a piece of cabbage leaf and eat like a wrap or small taco. Qawarma can substituted be with minced beef or lamb.

Dried chickpeas can be substituted with one tin of chickpeas, drained.

DIFFICULTY: ★★

•KIBBEH   •PASTRIES   •STEWS   •SWEETS   •TABBOULEH   •VEGAN   •VEGETARIAN   •WHEAT FREE   •WILD EDIBLE PLANTS

SPRING **MAIN DISHES**

SERVES: 4

زنكل عحامض

ZINKOL A HAMOD
LEMON ZINKOL

On Easter Friday, some villages may substitute the lemon juice with vinegar or add vinegar to the stew – a symbolic reference to Christ's drinking of vinegar.

2 onions, chopped

2 tsp olive oil

3 garlic cloves, crushed

4 cups/1l water

ZINKOL BALLS

1 cup/225g brown burghul (bulgur wheat), fine

1¾ cups/210g plain flour

1 tsp seven spices

1 cup/250ml water

½ cup/90g dried chickpeas, boiled and peeled

¾ cup/60ml freshly squeezed lemon juice

½ tsp sumac

1. In a large pan fry the onions in the oil over a medium heat until golden brown. Add the garlic and sauté for a minute more. Pour in the water, turn up the heat and bring to a boil. Simmer for 15 minutes over a medium heat.

2. To make the zinkol balls, put the burghul in a large mixing bowl. Sprinkle the flour and spices on top of burghul. Mix well. Gradually add cold water while mixing by hand. Knead well until the dough has a medium consistency. If the dough is too sticky add a little bit more flour. Leave to stand for 10 minutes. Form into marble sized balls (approximately 1 centimeter).

3. Gently drop the zinkol balls into boiling water. Cook for about 15 minutes without stirring. Add the chickpeas and continue cooking on a high heat for 10 minutes. Add the lemon juice and sumac and cook for 1 more minute. Serve hot in a tureen or deep bowl.

DIFFICULTY: ★★

•KIBBEH   •PASTRIES   •STEWS   •SWEETS   •TABBOULEH   •VEGAN   •VEGETARIAN   •WHEAT FREE   •WILD EDIBLE PLANTS

SHOUF

**SHOUF
KHREYBEH**

SALIM EL ASHKAR

Salim is waiting for us outside the gate of his 200-year-old family home, his warm smile as welcoming as the open doorway. He is very proud of the renovations and additions he has made since I stayed here last, and he has transformed the lower level into a guesthouse. It's one of my favourites. All three recipes he prepared that day had burghul (bulgur wheat) as an ingredient. "Because rice was not readily available in the mountain villages, burghul was the main staple and so most of the old traditional recipes have it," he explains. Burghul is an ingredient in all types of kibbeh, tabbouleh and kishk and is a staple in most village winter pantries.

ALL SEASON **APPETIZERS, SIDE DISHES**
SERVES: 10

كبّة بطاطا بيت الأشقر
KIBBET BATATA BEIT EL ASHKAR
BEIT EL ASHKAR'S POTATO KIBBEH

1½kg potatoes, peeled
2¼ cups/500g dark burghul (bulgur wheat), fine
1 onion, peeled
¼ cup/50g fresh marjoram
¼ cup/50g fresh basil
1 tsp cinnamon powder
½ tsp black pepper
1 tsp seven spices
1 cup/250 ml sunflower oil
Salt

1. Boil the potatoes in a large pan of salted water until soft. Drain, then mash thoroughly and set aside to cool.

2. Grate the onion into a mixing bowl and strain through a sieve. Discard the liquid.

3. In a pestle and mortar crush the marjoram and basil together with 55g of the burghul. Add the herbs and burghul mix to the mashed potatoes. Then add the onion and the rest of the burghul, oil and spices. Slowly add 250ml of boiling water and knead well until all ingredients are well combined. Add salt to taste. Scoop out a walnut-size portion of the dough and roll it into a ball of around 4–5cm diameter.

4. Serve in individual portions or in a shallow serving dish. Eat with bread and freshly cut spring onions.

DIFFICULTY: ★

•KIBBEH   •PASTRIES   •STEWS   •SWEETS   •TABBOULEH   •VEGAN   •VEGETARIAN   •WHEAT FREE   •WILD EDIBLE PLANTS

ALL SEASON **MAIN DISHES**

SERVES: 10

منسوفة حمّص
MANSOUFET HOMMOS
CHICKPEA MANSOUF

½ cup/50g sumac

3 cups/750ml cold water

1kg onions, chopped

2 tbsp vegetable oil

2 cups/350g dried chickpeas

2 cups/450g dark burghul (bulgar wheat), fine

¾ cup/85g plain flour

1 tsp 7 spices

1. Soak the sumac in 2 cups/500ml of the water for at least 30 minutes. Then strain, reserving the liquid for later. If a more tart taste is desired soak in only 1 cup/250ml of the water.

2. Sauté the onions in the oil until golden. Set aside.

3. To make the dough crush the chickpeas in a pestle and mortar until reduced to small pieces (see photo above). Add the burghul, flour and spices and mix well. Add 250ml of the water and knead by hand. Shape into 3cm patties and place on a baking tray.

4. Bring 2 litres of water to the boil in a large pan and add 2 tbsp of salt. Add the sautéed onions and cook for 5 minutes. Carefully drop the patties into the water and boil for 10 minutes without stirring. Add the sumac-infused water, stir gently, and cook for another 5 minutes. Remove from the heat, cover and let stand for 15 minutes before serving.

DIFFICULTY: ★★★

•KIBBEH   •PASTRIES   •STEWS   •SWEETS   •TABBOULEH   •VEGAN   •VEGETARIAN   •WHEAT FREE   •WILD EDIBLE PLANTS

ALL SEASON **APPETIZERS, SIDE DISHES**

SERVES: 10

تبّوله شتويّه
TABBOULEH SHATAWIYYEH
WINTER TABBOULEH

3 cups/500g dried chickpeas, soaked in a bowl of water overnight

1½ litres water

½ small white cabbage, outer leaves removed

1 large onion, chopped

100g minced beef

½ tsp cinnamon powder

½ tsp black pepper powder

½ tsp seven spices

2 cups/450g burghul (bulgur wheat), fine

1. Peel off the skins of the chickpeas and add to a large pan of boiling water. Boil them over a medium heat until just cooked, making sure they are not too soft. Drain the chickpeas and set aside.

2. Boil the cabbage leaves in a large pan of water until tender. Drain and set aside.

3. In a deep, heavy-based pan sauté the onions until golden brown. Add the meat and spices to the pan and fry until the meat is completely brown. Add the drained chickpeas and water to the meat in the pan. Bring to the boil and then pour in the burghul, stirring until mixed together well. Turn off the heat and leave to stand for 5 minutes. Serve in a bowl or deep-serving platter.

4. Take each cabbage and roll into a tube. Place the tubes on a serving platter

NOTES

Tabbouleh Shatawiyyeh is eaten by placing a couple of the cabbage rolls on a plate and then a serving of the burghul mixture. You then cut a piece of cabbage and add a bit of the burghul for each mouthful.

DIFFICULTY: ★

•KIBBEH   •PASTRIES   •STEWS   •SWEETS   •TABBOULEH   •VEGAN   •VEGETARIAN   •WHEAT FREE   •WILD EDIBLE PLANTS

SPRING, WINTER **MAIN DISHES**

SERVES: 12

يخنة الفول بالبرغل
YAKHNET EL FOUL BIL BURGHUL
BURGHUL AND FAVA BEAN STEW

500g onions, chopped
½ cup/120 ml sunflower oil
200g minced beef
2kg broad beans, shelled
1½ litres water
1kg tomatoes, chopped
1 tsp ground cinnamon
1 tsp seven spices
1 tsp black pepper powder
2 tbsp tomato purée
900g burghul (bulgur wheat), coarse

1. Heat the sunflower oil in a heavy-based pan over a medium heat, add the onions and sauté until golden brown. Stir in the minced beef and fry until any liquid has evaporated. Add the beans and sauté over a low heat for 5 minutes. Pour in the water and boil on a high heat, uncovered for 30 minutes.

2. Add the chopped tomatoes to a large mixing bowl and sprinkle all the spices over them. Mix the tomatoes and spices together and add the spiced tomatoes to the pan with the meat and beans. Bring to the boil again, turn down the heat and simmer for a further ten minutes.

3. Add the burghul to the pan, bring to the boil and simmer for two minutes over a medium heat. Turn off the heat, cover and leave to stand for another two minutes before serving.

DIFFICULTY: ★

•KIBBEH   •PASTRIES   •STEWS   •SWEETS   •TABBOULEH   •VEGAN   •VEGETARIAN   •WHEAT FREE   •WILD EDIBLE PLANTS

ALL SEASON MAIN DISHES

SERVES: 8

SHAMAHLIYYEH BIL BAYD
YOGHURT POACHED EGGS

750g onions, chopped
¾ cup/150ml sunflower oil
200g minced beef
1½ tsp cinnamon powder
2kg yoghurt
60g cornflour
3 cups/750ml water
12 eggs

1. Fry the onions in the oil in a large heavy-based pan until translucent. Stir in the meat and cook over a high heat until brown. Sprinkle cinnamon over the meat and stir well. Turn off the heat while preparing the yoghurt mix.

2. Mix the cornflour with 250ml of the water in a small bowl until the cornflour is completely dissolved. Pour the yoghurt into a large mixing bowl and stir in the cornflour solution. Add the remaining 500ml of water and mix everything together.

3. Add the yoghurt to the pan with the meat, stir well and turn up to a high heat. Bring to the boil. Crack the eggs, one by one, over the boiling yoghurt taking care to drop the eggs in different spots. Simmer over a medium heat for 3 minutes without stirring. Leave to stand for 5 minutes before serving.

NOTES
This is basically poaching the eggs in the yoghurt, so the aim is to serve the eggs in a yoghurt sauce. Another option is to serve with rice.

DIFFICULTY: ★

•KIBBEH •PASTRIES •STEWS •SWEETS •TABBOULEH •VEGAN •VEGETARIAN •WHEAT FREE •WILD EDIBLE PLANTS

SHOUF
MAASSER EL SHOUF

ELISSAR TEMRAZ

"When I was newly married, I hated cooking," says Elissar, who recalls that the area was going through difficult financial times during the civil war and they had to settle for ingredients and alternatives that were different from what she had been used to growing up. Necessity pushed her to cook as a source of income and thanks to the Food Heritage Foundation and the Lebanon Mountain Trail Association it became lucrative. The positive feedback from her guests rekindled her love for cooking. "It made me so happy when a guest would say 'this is the best…'" Today, cooking is not only a job; it's a source of joy and pride. The additional income has also helped her make improvements and additions to her house so she can receive larger groups of guests.

Elissar is known for her *Fatayer Bi Yakteen* (pumpkin turnovers) but on my first visit she informed me that we wouldn't be able to do her signature specialty. "My pumpkins aren't ripe yet," she said very simply. So we did the courgette turnovers instead and left the pumpkin turnovers for a second visit. All of her ingredients come from her garden, including the onions and garlic.

Elissar's Qawarma: Qawarma is a staple food in most mountain villages. She used to raise her own sheep and feed them on Mulberry leaves.

ELISSAR'S GARDEN AND VEGETABLE PATCH
Elissar cooks seasonally. All the organically-grown vegetables she cooked that day came fresh from her garden, including the onions and garlic.

SUMMER **APPETIZERS**

MAKES: 6

فطاير بالكوسى
FATAYER BIL KOUSSA
COURGETTE TURNOVERS

PASTRY
3 cups/420g wholemeal flour
1 tsp dried yeast
2–2½ cups/250–375ml water
½ tsp salt
½ tsp granulated sugar
2 tbsp olive oil

COURGETTE FILLING
2 tbsp qawarma or vegetable oil
2 onions, chopped
3 large courgettes
1 tomato, chopped
¼ tsp ground cinnamon
1 tsp salt
¼ tsp black pepper

1. For the pastry, combine all the dry ingredients in a large bowl and mix in the oil thoroughly by hand. Pour in the water, bring everything together into a dough and knead until the dough is soft but still firm. Cover or wrap in clingfilm and leave to rest overnight in the refrigerator.

2. For the filling, coarsely grate the courgettes using the grater's largest holes. Melt the qawarma in a frying pan. Add the onions and gently fry until soft. Add the courgettes and stir until starting to soften, then add the tomatoes, spices and seasoning. When the mixture has cooked for 1 minute, place it in a sieve and leave to cool while any excess liquid drains away.

3. To make the turnovers, preheat oven to 240°C/450°F/gas mark 9. Divide the dough into 6 portions and make each portion into a ball. Dust each ball with flour and place on a floured surface. Roll out each ball into a thin circle about 2mm (⅒ inch) thick. Place about two tablespoons of filling in the centre. Moisten the edges with water and seal the sides to form a triangle (see photos). Place the pies on a well-oiled baking tray and bake for 15 minutes before flipping them to bake for a further 5 minutes so both sides are slightly browned.

Delicious hot or cold.

NOTES
Substituting oil for the qawarma will make the pastry suitable for vegetarians.

DIFFICULTY: ★★

•KIBBEH •PASTRIES •STEWS •SWEETS •TABBOULEH •VEGAN •VEGETARIAN •WHEAT FREE •WILD EDIBLE PLANTS

FILLING   DOUGH

STEPS

ALL SEASON **APPETIZERS**

MAKES: 12

فطاير باليقطين
FATAYER BI YAKTEEN
PUMPKIN TURNOVERS

PASTRY

3 cups/420g wholemeal flour

1 tsp dried yeast

2-2½ cups/250-375ml water

½ tsp salt

½ tsp granulated sugar

2 tbsp olive oil

PUMPKIN FILLING

3½lbs/1.5kg pumpkin de-seeded and peeled

2 tbsp vegetable oil

2 onions, chopped

3½oz/100g beef mince

2 tomatoes, chopped

1. For the pastry, combine all the dry ingredients in a large bowl and mix in the oil thoroughly by hand. Pour in the water, bring everything together into a dough and knead until the dough is soft but still firm. Cover or wrap in clingfilm and leave to rest overnight in the refrigerator.

2. For the filling, grate the raw pumpkin using the grater's largest holes. Place the grated pumpkin in a sieve to drain. Gently fry the onions until soft and starting to colour. Stir in the meat and spices and cook until the meat has browned and any liquid has evaporated.

Add the pumpkin and cook until the pumpkin has softened – probably about 30 minutes. Remove the pan from the heat and stir in the tomatoes, seasoning to taste. Place the mixture in a sieve and leave to cool, allowing any excess liquid to drain away.

3. To make the turnovers, preheat oven to 240°C/450°F/gas mark 9. Divide the dough into 6 portions and make each portion into a ball. Dust each ball with flour and place on a floured surface. Roll out each ball into a thin circle about 2mm (¹⁄₁₀inch) thick. Place about two tablespoons of filling in the centre. Moisten the edges with water and seal the sides to form a triangle (see photos). Place the pies on a well-oiled baking tray and bake for 15 minutes before flipping them to bake for a further 5 minutes so both sides are slightly browned.

Delicious hot or cold.

NOTES

This sister dish to Fatayer Bil Koussa has a beef element as part of the mix.

DIFFICULTY: ★★★

•KIBBEH   •PASTRIES   •STEWS   •SWEETS   •TABBOULEH   •VEGAN   •VEGETARIAN   •WHEAT FREE   •WILD EDIBLE PLANTS

ALL SEASON **MAIN DISHES**
SERVES: 8

مخلوطة

MAKHLOUTA
MIXED BEAN STEW

- 1 cup/200g dried kidney beans
- 1 cup/200g dried fava beans
- 1 cup/200g dried canellini beans
- 1 cup/200g dried chickpeas
- 1 tbsp vegetable oil
- 1 tbsp olive oil
- 2 large onions, roughly chopped
- 7oz/200g beef mince
- 2 tsp ground cumin
- 1 tsp ground cinnamon
- 1 tsp seven spice mix
- 1 tsp salt
- 1 cup/200g fine dark bulgur wheat
- 1 cup/200g brown lentils
- 4 cups/400g fresh runner beans
- 8.5 fl. oz/2.5 litres water

1. Soak the dried pulses overnight. You can soak the beans together but soak the chickpeas separately.

2. Heat the oils in a large saucepan. Add the onion and cook over a medium heat until softened. Stir in the beef mince and cook until browned, then add the spices and salt and cook for a further minute. Add all remaining ingredients except the chickpeas. Pour in the water, cover and bring to the boil over a high heat.

3. Lower the heat to medium and cook for 1 hour.

4. Add the chickpeas and cook for an additional 20 minutes.

NOTES
You can substitute or add any other kind of dried bean that you like, making sure you soak them overnight.

DIFFICULTY: ★

•KIBBEH   •PASTRIES   •STEWS   •SWEETS   •TABBOULEH   •VEGAN   •VEGETARIAN   •WHEAT FREE   •WILD EDIBLE PLANTS

ALL SEASON **MAIN DISHES**
SERVES: 10

شيشبرك بسمّاق

SHISH BARAK BI SUMAC
SHISH BARAK WITH SUMAC

DOUGH

1 cup/140g wholemeal flour

¼ tsp salt

¼ tsp sugar

1 tsp oil

½ cup/125ml water

FILLING

1 tbsp vegetable oil

1 tbsp olive oil

1 onion, chopped

3.5oz/100g beef mince

½ tsp ground cinnamon

½ tsp black pepper

¼ tsp salt

¼ cup/30g walnuts, chopped

2 tbsp pine nuts

SAUCE

2 tbsp qawarma or olive oil

1 onion, chopped

¼ cup/50g basmati rice

½ cup/85g pre-cooked or drained tinned chickpeas

1½ pints/1 litre water

1 tbsp sumac

1. To make the dough, mix all dry ingredients in a large bowl and mix the oil in thoroughly by hand. Gradually add the water as you continue to knead until you have a soft, firm dough. Cover or wrap in clingfilm and leave to rest overnight in refrigerator.

2. To make the filling, heat the oils in a large frying pan and gently fry the onion until soft. Stir in the beef, cinnamon and seasoning and fry until well browned. Add the walnuts and pine nuts, cook for a further minute, then set aside, allowing to cool to room temperature.

3. Preheat oven to 350°F/180°C.

4. To make the shish barak, first dust the worksurface with flour. Roll out the dough thinly to about 2mm (1/10 inch) thick. Cut the dough into circles that are about 1½ inches/4cm wide using a cookie cutter or a small glass. Place one of the rounds in the palm of your hand and spoon a generous amount of the filling into the middle. Dampen the edges with water, fold the round in half and press the edges together to seal firmly. Bring the two pointed ends together and seal, like tortellini, and place on a greased baking tray. Bake until the shish barak parcels are slightly golden.

5. For the sauce, heat the qawarma or oil in a medium saucepan then fry the onion over a medium heat until slightly golden. Add the rice, chickpeas and water and simmer for about 10 minutes or until the rice is cooked. Carefully add all of the shish barak parcels and continue to simmer for 5 minutes. Add the sumac and continue to cook until the shish barak parcels are cooked *al dente*.

DIFFICULTY: ★★★

•KIBBEH   •PASTRIES   •STEWS   •SWEETS   •TABBOULEH   •VEGAN   •VEGETARIAN   •WHEAT FREE   •WILD EDIBLE PLANTS

ALL SEASON **DESSERTS**

MAKES: 60

حلاوة لوحيّه

HALAWAH LAWHIYYEH
LAWHIYYEH COOKIES

3 cups/420g wholemeal flour
2 tbsp butter
1 cup/115g roughly chopped walnuts
3 cups/700g grape molasses
¼ cup/25g sesame seeds

1. Lightly brown the flour in a baking tin over a gentle heat, stirring continuously so the flour does not burn. Add the butter and stir in until melted and thoroughly mixed with the flour. Reduce the heat to very low and stir in the walnuts. Remove pan from the heat and stir in the grape molasses by hand. Take care, as the mixture will be hot – it needs to be hot so you can shape the cookies. Elissar dips her hands under cold running water a couple of times as she does it to help keep them cool.

2. Flatten the dough in the tin to form an even layer and sprinkle over the sesame seeds, pressing them into the dough.

3. Leave to cool a little and cut into 2cm (¾inch) squares.

DIFFICULTY: ★

•KIBBEH   •PASTRIES   •STEWS   •SWEETS   •TABBOULEH   •VEGAN   •VEGETARIAN   •WHEAT FREE   •WILD EDIBLE PLANTS

SHOUF
MROSTI

BASSIMA ZEIDAN

The beautiful young girl with big blue eyes and long, shiny, chestnut coloured hair waiting for us in the town square is Malaak, Bassima's granddaughter. Malaak means angel in Arabic, and she is certainly angelic. I am also a bit perplexed when I meet Bassima. She looks way too young to be a grandmother.

"I have five sisters and two brothers," Bassima tells me. "When I was nine, my parents had to take me out of school to stay home and make the bread for my family because my mother was very ill and we were poor. From her bed, she gave me the instructions and, slowly, I learnt how to grind the wheat, make the dough and cook it on the iron dome of the *saj* grill that is a fixture in most Lebanese rural homes. At first, the bread wasn't good, but my mother was patient and eventually I understood and perfected the process. I have never bought bread from a bakery."

Her *marqouq* (a paper thin flat bread) is the best I have ever tasted. Married at 15, she also taught herself how to cook and today she is Mrosti's authority on food preparation and cooking. When we sat down for her delicious meal of wild, edible plant dishes, made with hindbeh (wild chicory), akkoub (gundelia), ors anneh (eryngo) and mesheh (salsify). She served us with warmth and generosity as large as her radiant smile.

SPRING **APPETIZERS, SIDE DISHES**

SERVES: 6

هندبه باللّبنه

HINDBEH BI LABNEH
WILD CHICORY WITH YOGHURT SAUCE

1 garlic clove
2 cups/500g labneh
2 cups/500g water
⅓ cup/80ml olive oil
500g cucumber, sliced in half and chopped
250g hindbeh, chopped
1 cup/25g mint, chopped

1. Grate the garlic clove into a mixing bowl. Add the labneh and water. Then mix with a whisk until well blended.

2. Add the olive oil and cucumbers to the labneh and mix well. Stir in the hindbeh and mint.

3. Serve in a bowl with a drizzle of olive oil.

TO MAKE LABNEH
Place a large coffee filter in a sieve on top of a large bowl. Pour in a tub of plain yoghurt. Cover and keep in the refrigerator overnight. The strained yoghurt remaining in the coffee filter the following day (labneh) should be the consistency of cream cheese.

NOTES
Wild chicory (hindbeh) can be substituted with regular chicory but the leaves should be tender.

DIFFICULTY: ★

•KIBBEH •PASTRIES •STEWS •SWEETS •TABBOULEH •VEGAN •VEGETARIAN •WHEAT FREE •WILD EDIBLE PLANTS

ALL SEASON **APPETIZERS, SIDE DISHES**

SERVES: 6

متبّل يقطين

MTABBAL YAKTEEN
PUMPKIN TAHINI DIP

1 medium sized pumpkin, peeled and cut into large cubes
¼ cup/60ml lemon juice
¾ cup/200g tahini
1 garlic, crushed
olive oil
salt to taste

Boil the pumpkin cubes in a large pan of water until very soft. Strain well, transfer to a large mixing bowl and purée until smooth. In a small bowl mix the tahini with the lemon juice and garlic. Add the tahini mix to the mashed pumpkin and mix well. Add salt to taste. Serve with a drizzle of olive oil.

DIFFICULTY: ★

•KIBBEH •PASTRIES •STEWS •SWEETS •TABBOULEH •VEGAN •VEGETARIAN •WHEAT FREE •WILD EDIBLE PLANTS

DEIR EL QAMAR, SHOUF

Akkoub (gundelia) is a spiny, thistle-like plant that is foraged in the mountain highlands. It is considered a delicacy and has a taste similar to artichoke. Akkoub peelers love company and it is common to find them hard at work with a pot of coffee at hand and a bit of town gossip to lighten the task.

SPRING **APPETIZERS**

MAKES: 50

KIBBET AKKOUB
GUNDELIA KIBBEH

KIBBEH DOUGH

250g akkoub/gundelia stalks, cleaned

4 cups/1kg burghul (bulgur wheat)

250g semolina

1 cup/125g cornflour

1 tbsp dried marjoram

1 tbsp dried basil

1 tsp cinnamon

1 tsp seven spices

1 tbsp kibbeh spices

1 onion, grated

zest of 1 lemon

FILLING

500g potatoes, boiled with skin on

½ cup/65g walnuts, coarsely chopped

⅛ tsp chilli powder (optional)

2 tbsp sunflower oil

½ cup/200g qawarma, (substitute with 200g browned minced beef)

DIFFICULTY: ★★★★

1. To make the kibbeh dough, over a high heat boil the akkoub stalks in 7 cups/1½ litres of salted water in a large heavy based pan until well cooked (soft). Strain and reserve the cooking liquid. Soak the burghul and semolina in 3 cups/750ml of the reserved liquid for 30 minutes in a large mixing bowl. Add all the remaining kibbeh dough ingredients, along with the drained akkoub stalks to the bowl after the 30 minutes and knead together, adding more of the cooking liquid until the dough can be easily shaped (around 3-4 cups/750ml more of water).

2. For the filling peel the boiled potatoes and grate coarsely into a large bowl. Add all the remaining ingredients and mix by hand. Divide and shape into individual portions of filling and place on a tray, (photo page 140).

3. In a small bowl dissolve 1 tbsp salt and 1 tbsp cornflour in 1 cup/250ml of cold water. This will be used for shaping the kibbeh balls.

4. To shape and fill the kibbeh balls, dip fingers in the cornflour solution and smooth over hands to prevent sticking.
1. Shape the dough into a ping pong sized ball (photo 1 on following spread).
2. Hollow out (photo 2).
3. Place the filling in the hollow and close (photo 3).
4. Shape as in photo 4, smoothing surface with the cornflour water.

5. Deep fry the kibbeh balls in hot oil until lightly browned. Place on paper towels to absorb excess oil.

NOTES
There are no substitutes for gundelia.

•KIBBEH •PASTRIES •STEWS •SWEETS •TABBOULEH •VEGAN •VEGETARIAN •WHEAT FREE •WILD EDIBLE PLANTS

BASSIMA'S WAY OF STUFFING KIBBEH

FILLING

DOUGH

SPRING, SUMMER **SIDE DISHES**

SERVES: 4

تبّولة بالعدس
TABBOULEH BIL ADASS
LENTIL TABBOULEH

1 onion, chopped

¼ cup/60ml olive oil

¼ tsp ground cinnamon

1 cup/200g red lentils, soaked overnight in water, then drained

2 cups/50g fresh parsley, chopped

2 tomatoes, chopped

1 cup/25g fresh mint, chopped

¼ cup/60ml lemon juice

½ tsp salt

1 tsp tomato puree

chilli powder, to taste

1. In a small bowl, mix the onion, cinnamon and oil. Leave to steep for 15 minutes.

2. Mix all the remaining ingredients in a large bowl. Add the infused onion mixture, stir all the ingredients together and serve immediately.

RECOMMENDATION

To be eaten with fresh vine leaves when in season. Otherwise with romaine lettuce leaves.

DIFFICULTY: ★★

•KIBBEH •PASTRIES •STEWS •SWEETS •TABBOULEH •VEGAN •VEGETARIAN •WHEAT FREE •WILD EDIBLE PLANTS

SPRING **SIDE DISHES**
SERVES: 8

تبّولة قرصعنّه
TABBOULET ORS ANNEH
ERYNGO TABBOULEH

1 onion, chopped

¼ tsp ground cinnamon

1 tsp salt

2 tbsp olive oil

½ cup lemon juice

250g ors anneh (eryngo), washed and chopped

1 cup/25g fresh mint, chopped

1kg tomatoes, chopped

1 tsp pomegranate molasses

10 cabbage leaves, whole leaves lightly blanched in boiling water

1. Put the chopped onions in a small bowl. Sprinkle with cinnamon and salt. Stir in olive oil and lemon juice and leave to infuse while preparing the other ingredients.

2. In a large mixing bowl mix the ors anneh, mint and tomatoes by hand. Add the onion and lemon-oil mix, along with pomegranate molasses and mix well.

3. Serve with the lightly-blanched cabbage leaves on the side.

NOTES

There is no substitute for eryngo.

Substitute pomegranate molasses with balsamic vinegar if desired.

DIFFICULTY: ★

•KIBBEH •PASTRIES •STEWS •SWEETS •TABBOULEH •VEGAN •VEGETARIAN •WHEAT FREE •WILD EDIBLE PLANTS

SPRING **APPETIZERS, SIDE DISHES**

SERVES: 6

مغمورة مشّه
MAGHMOURAT MISHEH
SALSIFY PILAF

3 cups/500g chickpeas
1 onion, chopped
⅓ cup/80ml sunflower oil
2 cups/500g misheh (salsify), chopped coarsely
¼ tsp ground cinnamon
4 cups/1l water

1. Cover the chickpeas with about 6cm of cold water in a large bowl and soak overnight. Peel and strain.

2. In a heavy-based pan, fry the onion in the sunflower oil over a medium heat until golden. Stir in the chickpeas and spices and sauté for 1 minute. Add the water and bring to the boil, then simmer covered for 30 minutes.

3. Add the misheh to the chickpea mixture and cook for a further 20 minutes or until the misheh is soft, stirring gently at regular intervals.

4. Serve the pilaf on a shallow serving dish.

NOTES
There is no substitute for salsify/misheh.

DIFFICULTY: ★★

•KIBBEH •PASTRIES •STEWS •SWEETS •TABBOULEH •VEGAN •VEGETARIAN •WHEAT FREE •WILD EDIBLE PLANTS

SPRING **MAIN DISHES**

SERVES: 6

مقلوبة عكّوب

MAKLOUBET AKKOUB
GUNDELIA PILAF

- 500g meat (lamb or beef), cut into small, bite size cubes
- 2 cups/350g rice
- ¼ cup/50ml and 2 tbsp vegetable oil
- 4 cups/1l water
- 2 cups/500g akkoub, stems and bulbs
- 1kg aubergine, cut into small cubes
- 1 tomato, grated
- 1 tsp ground cinnamon
- 1 tsp seven spices
- ⅛ tsp chilli powder, optional
- 2 tbsp salt

1. In a heavy-based casserole fry the meat cubes in the 2 tablespoons of vegetable oil over a high heat until browned. Add 2 cups/500ml of the water, turn down to a medium heat and simmer for 30 minutes until well done.

2. Soak the rice in a bowl of hot water with 1 tsp of salt for 15 minutes. Strain.

3. Cut the akkoub into large pieces. Deep fry the akkoub until lightly golden and place on paper towels to absorb any excess oil. Do the same with the aubergine.

4. Add the akkoub, aubergine and tomato to the boiled meat and continue to cook for a further 5 minutes.

5. Sauté the rice in the 50ml of vegetable oil. Add the spices and salt until all of the rice is well coated. Lower heat on the meat and vegetables. Spoon the fried rice evenly over the meat and vegetables. Do not stir.

6. Gently drizzle the remaining water over the rice. Bring to the boil, then continue cooking for 15 minutes or until the rice is done.

DIFFICULTY: ★

•KIBBEH •PASTRIES •STEWS •SWEETS •TABBOULEH •VEGAN •VEGETARIAN •WHEAT FREE •WILD EDIBLE PLANTS

SPRING **MAIN DISHES**
SERVES: 8

مشّه بالقورما

MISHEH BIL QAWARMA
SALSIFY WITH QAWARMA

3 cups/525g basmati rice
1 onion, chopped
¼ cup/240ml sunflower oil
¼ cup/60g qawarma
300g minced beef
½ tsp cinnamon
½ tsp seven spices
½kg misheh (salsify), coarsely chopped
6 cups/1½l water

1. Soak the rice in water for 15 minutes. Rinse and strain.

2. In a frying pan fry the onion in a tablespoon of the oil over a medium heat until golden.

3. Brown the minced beef in a large heavy-based pan with two tablespoons of the oil and transfer to a plate. Then brown the qawarma in the same pan with another two tablespoons of oil and add to the beef. Sauté the beef, qawarma and onion with the spices in the rest of the oil over a medium heat in the same pan for five minutes. Add the misheh and stir. Cook until the misheh is half cooked, around 10 minutes. Add the water and cook for another 10 minutes. Stir in the rice. Cover and cook for 15 minutes on a low heat. Do not stir the rice too often.

DIFFICULTY: ★★

•KIBBEH •PASTRIES •STEWS •SWEETS •TABBOULEH •VEGAN •VEGETARIAN •WHEAT FREE •WILD EDIBLE PLANTS

THE SOUTH

THE SOUTH
HASBAYA

WAFAA SHMEISS

Food "trends" these days encourage us to buy local, eat organic, choose seasonal and seek out the so-called superfoods. Thus, the enlightened foodie strives to live by this creed for a healthier life and tastier food experience. The Arabs, who have a phrase for everything, might call this reinventing the wheel (or 'gunpowder' in Arabic). We've been doing it forever! Wafaa Shmeiss might agree. She, along with her family, has been practicing this "trendy" way of life for generations. In fact, it's all she knows. When I asked her how she decides what to cook in the morning she says, "I walk out to my vegetable patch and we eat whatever is ready to be picked."

Indeed, there are very few vegetable stores in Hasbaya. People grow and forage most of their own produce and make their own preserved winter food or *mouneh*.

Wafaa's kitchen is full of smiles and warmth. Sister-in-law Nada is her bubbly *sous chef,* who firmly believes that food tastes better when cooked with love. On the menu is *maash,* or mung bean. But how did a grain, predominantly from South East Asia, end up being cultivated on the foothills of Mount Hermon? We asked her where she buys it and she said that they have been growing it in the hills around Hasbaya since before her grandfather was born. The locals, especially the elderly villagers, believe it makes you sturdy and strong – "the nails of the knees" as they say in these parts, according to Wafaa. No wonder there are more than a few centenarians in Hasbaya.

ALL SEASON APPETIZERS

SERVES: 12

كبة بطاطا بالملفوف

KIBBET BATATA BIL MALFOUF
POTATO KIBBEH WITH CABBAGE LEAVES

KIBBEH SPICES

equal quantities of ground marjoram, cinnamon, cardamom, cloves

6 cups/½kg fine burghul (bulgur wheat)
1½ tsp kibbeh spices
¼ cup/125ml water
2 onions, finely chopped
1 cup/240ml olive oil
½ white cabbage
½kg potatoes, peeled and cut into cubes
1 cup olive oil

1. Rinse the burghul in a colander with water. Transfer to a bowl and mix in the spices. Add the water and set aside to absorb the water.

2. Fry the onions in olive oil over a low heat until soft.

3. Coarsely chop the cabbage and soak in a large bowl of cold water. Add to a pan of salted boiling water. Bring to the boil and cook for 10 minutes over a high heat. Drain and set aside.

4. Boil the potatoes in a large pan of salted water until soft enough to be mashed. Drain and reserve the cooking liquid. Mash the potatoes until smooth. Add the potatoes to the burghul along with two tablespoons of their cooking water and mix well. Let the mixture rest for a few minutes, adding the cooking water a tablespoon at a time until the burghul is soft. Mix in the onions.

5. Serve hot in a shallow platter with the cabbage on the side.

DIFFICULTY: ★

•KIBBEH •PASTRIES •STEWS •SWEETS •TABBOULEH •VEGAN •VEGETARIAN •WHEAT FREE •WILD EDIBLE PLANTS

FALL, SUMMER **SIDE DISHES**

SERVES: 10

مسقّعة الباذنحان
MOUSSAKAT BATINJEN
AUBERGINE MOUSSAKA

1¼ cups/250g dried chickpeas, soaked overnight
½kg onions, sliced
½ cup/120ml olive oil
1 cup/250ml water
2kg small aubergines, peeled
1kg tomatoes, pureed
¼ tsp salt

1. Drain, rinse and peel the chickpeas. In a heavy-based pan sauté the onions in the oil over a low heat until they are soft. Add the chickpeas and continue to cook, covered on a low heat for 15 minutes. Add the water. Cook until the chickpeas are soft.

2. Cut the peeled aubergines into cubes. Add to the pan. Partially cover and cook on a low heat for 10 minutes. Add the tomatoes and salt to taste. Cook until the sauce is reduced and thickened.

NOTES
If your aubergines are small and guaranteed to have been picked that day, you can save the stems. Scrape off the prickly part and add to the onion and chickpeas before adding water.

DIFFICULTY: ★

•KIBBEH •PASTRIES •STEWS •SWEETS •TABBOULEH •VEGAN •VEGETARIAN •WHEAT FREE •WILD EDIBLE PLANTS

FALL, WINTER MAIN DISHES

SERVES: 6

MAASH
MUNG BEAN SOUP

½kg dried mung beans
2 red onions, sliced
¼ cup/60ml olive oil
4 bay leaves
¼ tsp ground cinnamon
¼ tsp ground cardamom
¼ tsp ground cloves
¼ tsp black pepper powder
Toasted pitta bread

Separate the impurities from the mung beans and wash well in a colander. Place the beans in a large saucepan and add water until the beans are covered. Add the sliced onions and all the spices. Cook with a lid on until the beans are soft (about 30 minutes).

NOTES
You can add coarse burghul (bulgur wheat) with the beans at the start.

Serve with turnip pickles and the toasted pitta bread cut into squares. Add a squeeze of fresh lemon to taste.

DIFFICULTY: ★

•KIBBEH •PASTRIES •STEWS •SWEETS •TABBOULEH •VEGAN •VEGETARIAN •WHEAT FREE •WILD EDIBLE PLANTS

ALL SEASON **MAIN DISHES**

SERVES: 8

مغربية دجاج بالخزامى

MOUGHRABIET DJEJ BIL KHOZAMI
CHICKEN MOUGHRABIEH WITH LAVENDER

500g dried chickpeas, soaked overnight (or 4 tins of chickpeas, drained)

1l water

500g onions, sliced

2 bay leaves

⅛ tsp cinnamon powder

1½kg chicken pieces – thighs and drumsticks

1 tbsp plain flour

1 tsp vinegar

50g lavender powder (or lavender flowers ground in a pestle and mortar)

25g cinnamon sticks

2 whole cardamom pods

3 cloves

½ tsp black peppercorns

6 cups/500g moughrabieh

1½ tsp olive oil

¾ tbsp butter

A pinch of salt

1. Boil the chickpeas in ½ litre of water with half of the onions, half the bay leaves and a pinch of the cinnamon powder. Cook until just done – *al dente*.

2. Rub the chicken pieces with the flour, salt and vinegar. Leave for 10 minutes. After the ten minutes rinse and pat the pieces dry. Boil the chicken in a large saucepan of water over a high heat, frequently removing any scum that forms for ten minutes. Take out the chicken pieces with a slotted spoon and discard the water. Fill another pan with ½ litre of water and add the remaining onions and all the spices apart from the cinnamon powder (including the ones wrapped in the cloth). Add the chicken pieces and cook for a further 30 minutes.

3. Add the chicken pieces and their cooking water to the pot of chickpeas. Add 25g of the lavender and cook for a further 15 minutes.

4. Boil the moughrabieh *(see below)* in a large pan of water with the olive oil, butter and salt until fully cooked, slightly more than al dente. Drain in a colander and rinse with cold water. Rub with the lavender and the remaining cinnamon powder.

5. Serve the moughrabieh in a shallow dish accompanied by the chicken and chickpea stew in a deep bowl or tureen.

NOTES

Moughrabieh, also known as 'Lebanese couscous,' can be bought fresh or frozen in Lebanon, but families make it at home – a lengthy process. In a double boiler (or use a colander over a pan of water), steam over the chicken broth until done. Cover with *markouk* bread to keep warm.

DIFFICULTY: ★★★★★

•KIBBEH   •PASTRIES   •STEWS   •SWEETS   •TABBOULEH   •VEGAN   •VEGETARIAN   •WHEAT FREE   •WILD EDIBLE PLANTS

ALL SEASON **DESSERTS**

MAKES: 24 SMALL BOWLS

RIZ BI DEBS
GRAPE MOLASSES RICE PUDDING

½kg Italian rice (eg. Arborio)
1l water
1 cup/260g grape molasses
4 tbsp orange blossom water
3 cups/750ml water
Walnuts or almonds for decoration

1. Add the rice to the water in a large non-stick pan, stirring continuously over a low heat until totally soft. Add the grape molasses and continue stirring until very sticky. Stir the orange blossom water into the rice and remove from the heat.

2. Serve in small bowls or glasses and sprinkle with walnuts or almonds on top.

NOTES
This dessert is quite sweet and so serving in small individual portions is recommended.

Carob molasses can be substituted for grape molasses.

DIFFICULTY: ★

•KIBBEH   •PASTRIES   •STEWS   •SWEETS   •TABBOULEH   •VEGAN   •VEGETARIAN   •WHEAT FREE   •WILD EDIBLE PLANTS

ALL SEASONS **DESSERTS**
MAKES: 36

كعك بالخزامى
KAAK BIL KHOZAMI
KAAK WITH LAVENDER

5 cups/600g wholemeal flour
½ tsp lavender powder
2 cups/450g granulated sugar
2 tbsp baking powder
1 cup/160g semolina flour
1 tsp cardamom powder
2 cups/250g powdered milk
3 cups/750ml water
250g butter
1 cup/140g sesame seeds
1 tbsp olive oil

1. Preheat oven to 200°C/400°F/gas mark 6. Grease all baking trays with olive oil.

2. To make the kaak cookies combine all the dry ingredients apart from the powdered milk and sesame seeds, in a large mixing bowl. Add the powdered milk and water (or fresh milk). Mix together by hand. The dough will be soft and sticky. Cover and let rest for 15 minutes. Place a small bowl of olive oil near you. Shape the dough into balls. Regularly dip fingers into the bowl of oil and coat the palm of hand with oil while shaping the dough balls. For each kaak sprinkle sesame seeds onto a board and press each ball into the sesame seeds to form a patty shape 2cm thick or, if using a mould, sprinkle the sesame seeds into mould and press the dough balls into the mould so the upper side is flat. Place the moulded dough shapes on the baking trays with the sesame seed side facing up and, if using the mould, turn out onto the baking trays. Leave a 2cm space between each kaak.

3. Cook for 12 minutes until golden. Remove the baking trays from the oven and place on a cooling rack.

4. The cookies can be stored in an airtight container for up to two weeks.

NOTES
You can substitute the powdered milk and water with 3 cups/750ml fresh milk.

DIFFICULTY: ★★★
•KIBBEH   •PASTRIES   •STEWS   •SWEETS   •TABBOULEH   •VEGAN   •VEGETARIAN   •WHEAT FREE   •WILD EDIBLE PLANTS

THE SOUTH
MARJEYOUN

FERIAL & MAJED MAKHOUL

There is a sad thing happening in Marjeyoun. The population has been shrinking since the liberation of South Lebanon from the Israeli Army in 2000 and the number of people in the town has shrunk by 75%. Along with the soldiers, the youth has also gone, as have many young families, and it was against this unfortunate backdrop that Ferial and Majed had to make the tough decision to close their once thriving Arabic sweet shop. But since they both loved cooking and baking they decided to downscale it to a bakery instead. The new business is faring a bit better but the couple still struggles.

Ferial comes from a family of sweet makers and the olive groves they cultivated have been in the family for generations. I mention to Majed that I hear the best olive oil in Lebanon comes from Deir Mimass, a neighbouring border village. He disappears into the next room as Ferial finishes the last dish of *Brikat* (page 238) and reappears bearing two bottles of the golden liquid. "THIS is the best olive oil in Lebanon and it comes from our groves," he beams. It must surely be this pride, passion and generosity of spirit that lie at the heart of the wonderful meal we enjoyed together that evening.

Ferial and Majed's life is one of resilience and survival, ever ready to adapt to change. They both love cooking; serving and feeding their customers is their joy. Ferial learnt cooking from her mother, but Majed says she far surpassed her long ago. "She has *nafass* (breath)" he says. "She breathes love into her dishes."

FALL APPETIZERS

SERVES: 6

عدس بالشومر

ADASS BIL SHUMAR
LENTILS WITH FENNEL

½ cup/100g dried brown lentils
1kg fennel leaves, finely chopped
4-5 cups/1l-1.25l water
3 onions, chopped
½ cup/120ml olive oil
salt
1 lemon, sliced

1. Boil the lentils in a large pan with the water for 30 minutes. Add the fennel and cook for a further 20 minutes until the lentils and fennel are soft.

2. Sauté the onions in half of the olive oil in a frying pan over a medium heat until golden. Add the remainder of the oil to the onions, stir together and transfer to the pan of lentils. Cook for an additional 10 minutes or until the water has evaporated. Add salt to taste.

3. Serve in a shallow platter with the lemon slices as garnish.

DIFFICULTY: ★

•KIBBEH •PASTRIES •STEWS •SWEETS •TABBOULEH •VEGAN •VEGETARIAN •WHEAT FREE •WILD EDIBLE PLANTS

ALL SEASONS **APPETIZERS**
MAKES: 24

BRIKAT
WALNUT AND
EGG PIES

DOUGH

2 tbsp granulated sugar

1 tbsp salt

1 tsp dried yeast

4 cups/500g plain flour

1 cup/250ml warm water

FILLING

4 onions, chopped

½ cup/120ml olive oil

1½ cups/200g walnuts, chopped

8 eggs

½ tsp cinnamon powder

½ tsp ground black pepper

¼ tsp ground white pepper

1 tsp sumac (optional)

1. To make the dough, mix all the dry ingredients in a large mixing bowl. Gradually add warm water and combine by hand until the dough is medium-firm. Roll out the dough until thin. Cut out 5-6cm circles using a pastry cutter.

2. Pre-heat the oven to 200°C/400°F/gas mark 6.

3. To make the filling, fry the onion in the olive oil in a frying pan over a low heat until soft. Add the walnuts and stir for a minute. Crack the eggs on top of the onions and nuts. Sprinkle all the spices, apart from the sumac, on top of the eggs. Stir until the eggs are cooked. Sprinkle with sumac and remove from heat.

4. To fill and shape the pies, place a pastry circle on your hand and spray lightly with water (or run a wet finger over surface). Spoon about one tablespoon of filling into the centre. Run a wet finger round the rim of the circle and fold over to form a half moon. Then press the outer rims shut. Place the pies on a greased baking sheet. Brush each pie with oil and cook until golden brown for approximately 15 minutes.

NOTES

Sumac can be left out if not available

DIFFICULTY: ★★★

•KIBBEH   •PASTRIES   •STEWS   •SWEETS   •TABBOULEH   •VEGAN   •VEGETARIAN   •WHEAT FREE   •WILD EDIBLE PLANTS

SPRING, SUMMER **SIDE DISHES**
SERVES: 6

تبّولة فول
TABBOULET FOUL
FAVA BEAN TABBOULEH

- 3 large bunches parsley, chopped
- 1 cup/170g fresh fava/broad beans (if unavailable, use either dried chickpeas, soaked overnight, strained and peeled, or two tins of chickpeas)
- ½ cup/15g fresh mint, chopped
- 1 onion, finely chopped
- ½ cup/120g brown burghul, (bulgur wheat) coarse
- ½ cup/120ml olive oil
- 2 lemons, squeezed
- ¼ tsp seven spices

1. Soak the burghul in a bowl with one cup/250ml of water for 30 minutes. In another bowl sprinkle the seven spices over the finely chopped onion and gently rub into the onion.

2. When ready to serve the dish, mix all the ingredients together in a salad bowl and add salt to taste.

NOTES
Adding 2 chopped tomatoes is optional, but Ferial prefers her tabbouleh without them.

DIFFICULTY: ★★

•KIBBEH   •PASTRIES   •STEWS   •SWEETS   •TABBOULEH   •VEGAN   •VEGETARIAN   •WHEAT FREE   •WILD EDIBLE PLANTS

ALL SEASONS **MAIN DISHES**

SERVES: 16

ورق عنب و كوسى بالدجاج
WARAQ ENAB BIL DJEJ
STUFFED COURGETTES AND VINE LEAVES WITH CHICKEN

3kg chicken pieces, thighs and drumsticks, bone in
3 cinnamon sticks
6 bay leaves
6 cloves
1kg long grain rice, washed
1kg minced beef or lamb
½ tsp ground black pepper
½ tsp cinnamon powder
¼ tsp ground white pepper
2kg small courgettes, hollowed out
1kg vine leaves
1 cup/240ml olive oil
1 cup/240ml cooking oil

1. Brown the chicken pieces in oil and layer in the bottom of a deep pan with the cinnamon sticks, bay leaves and cloves.

2. For the stuffing, mix the rice with the meat. Add the ground spices and salt.

3. If using fresh vine leaves, blanch lightly and strain. If from a jar, rinse and strain before stuffing.

4. Stuff and roll vine leaves according to the photos on the following spread. Layer the stuffed vine leaves over the chicken making sure they are tightly packed. Stuff the hollowed-out courgettes and layer the courgettes on top. Add water to the level of the courgettes, but do not cover. Cook uncovered on a high heat until the water comes to the boil. Lower to a low heat and cook uncovered for about an hour until all are tender.

5. Place a glass bowl in the sink. Place a flat round plate over the pan and tilt the pan, and drain the excess liquid into the bowl, using the plate to hold back the vine leaves and courgettes. Place a flat round serving platter, inverted, on top of the pot. Say a prayer, and turn the pot upside-down so that the contents fall onto the serving platter.

DIFFICULTY: ★★★★

•KIBBEH •PASTRIES •STEWS •SWEETS •TABBOULEH •VEGAN •VEGETARIAN **•WHEAT FREE** •WILD EDIBLE PLANTS

STUFFED VINE LEAVES STEPS

STUFFED COURGETTES STEPS

245

THE SOUTH
ZAWTAR

IMM QASSEM & MUHAMMAD NEHME

THYME IN THE DEEP SOUTH

Muhammad looks like an actor that has been well-cast for his part in a movie. A combination of Ben Kingsley and Anthony Quinn, the mischievous glint in his eye and his witty retorts keep us on our toes. The playful tenderness between him and his wife, Imm Qassem, is lovely to watch and despite it being a rather patriarchal community, he knows better than to go into the kitchen when she's cooking in their home in Zawtar, a small farming village in South Lebanon.

During the Israeli occupation of South Lebanon, Muhammad's routine of foraging for wild thyme was made more difficult by having to dodge Israeli sniper fire. The abundant countryside had been transformed into a war zone. "I had a wife and four young children," he tells me. "I had to find a less dangerous way to find thyme."

So, he set out to do something no one had done before: cultivate wild thyme. His naturally analytical and scientific mind, combined with his creativity and determination, spurred him to success. He was also driven by an incident that had stayed with him from his youth.

In the 1940s a group of farmers with a vision for a better future for their children had visited an influential and wealthy politician with a proposal to establish a technical school for the area. He scoffed at them. Did they really believe that their peasant sons could amount to anything? After Muhammad's initial outrage and anger had reduced from a boil to a steady simmer, he knew that he would one day prove this man wrong. In spite of his own poor education, he was able to do something many agro-engineers had failed to do: grow wild thyme. In 2000 his successful endeavor was the seed that grew into Zaatar Zawtar, a thriving business that has opened financial opportunities for over twenty families in Zawtar and neighbouring villages.

Taking great pride in his packaged zaatar mix, he tells me he sources only the best ingredients. In addition to his own thyme, he gets his sumac from the highlands of the Shouf, the sea salt from Anfeh in the North and locally grown sesame seeds from nearby Marjeyoun. Zaatar Zawtar is one of the few producers of thyme that has Food and Drugs Administration approval and a license for export to the USA. But what Muhammad takes particular pride and gratification in is that all his children are educated and his only daughter is an engineer.

What Muhammad represents is not just a story of creativity, intelligence and grit. He stands for the spirit of man's first farmers - those who took the first steps toward settled agriculture. We owe them a lot.

Muhamad "Abou Qassem" Nehmeh only uses what he believes are the best ingredients for his Zaatar mix. They include home-grown wild thyme; locally-grown sesame seeds from Marjeyoun; sumac from the highlands of the Shouf in the centre of Lebanon; sea salt from Anfeh in the north of the country and a healthy dollop of passion and pride.

SPRING, SUMMER **APPETIZERS, SIDE DISHES**

SERVES: 10

كمّونه

KAMMOUNEH
FRESH HERB KIBBEH PASTE

FRESH INGREDIENTS
1/3 cup/10g fresh marjoram
1/3 cup/10g fresh parsley
1/3 cup/10g fresh basil leaves
1 onion, peeled and quartered
1 spring onion
1 otra leaf
1 green chilli pepper
1 tsp salt
¼ tsp hot chilli powder (optional)

DRIED INGREDIENTS
1 tsp dried wild rose petals (ward wultani)
1 tsp clove powder
2 tsp cinnamon powder
1 tsp cumin seeds
1 tsp grated nutmeg
1 tsp black pepper powder
1/3 cup/75g fine burghul (bulgur wheat)

1. Place all the fresh ingredients plus the burghul in a food processor. Blend well. Add the dry ingredients and blend again. You can, of course, adjust the amount of chilli powder according to taste.

2. To serve, place the kammouneh on a small serving dish. Drizzle with olive oil and eat with flatbread and the spring onions on the side.

DIFFICULTY: ★

•KIBBEH   •PASTRIES   •STEWS   •SWEETS   •TABBOULEH   **•VEGAN**   **•VEGETARIAN**   •WHEAT FREE   •WILD EDIBLE PLANTS

SPRING, SUMMER **SIDE DISHES**

SERVES: 4

FRAKEH
KIBBEH TARTAR

100g lean, finely minced beef
2 tbsp kammouneh (see page 250)
¼ cup/55g fine burghul (bulgur wheat)
¼ cup/60ml water
salt to taste

1. In a large bowl soak the burghul in the water for 10 minutes. Mix the beef and kammouneh together with your hands, add to the soaked burghul and mix together.

2. Serve on a platter immediately. Drizzle with olive oil and eat accompanied by bread of choice.

DIFFICULTY: ★

•KIBBEH •PASTRIES •STEWS •SWEETS •TABBOULEH •VEGAN •VEGETARIAN •WHEAT FREE •WILD EDIBLE PLANTS

SPRING, SUMMER **SIDE DISHES**

SERVES: 4

كبّة بندوره
KIBBET BANADOURA
TOMATO KIBBEH

1 cup/225g burghul (bulgur wheat)

3 large tomatoes, coarsely chopped

1 tbsp tomato purée

½ cup/120g kammouneh (see page 250)

Mix the burghul and kammouneh in a large bowl. Add the chopped tomatoes.

Leave for 10 minutes or until tomato liquid is absorbed by the burghul. Mix in the tomato purée. Place on a serving dish and drizzle with olive oil. Eat with bread of choice.

DIFFICULTY: ★

•KIBBEH   •PASTRIES   •STEWS   •SWEETS   •TABBOULEH   •VEGAN   •VEGETARIAN   •WHEAT FREE   •WILD EDIBLE PLANTS

SUMMER **APPETIZERS SIDE DISHES**

SERVES: 4

كبة بطاطا بالكمّونه
KIBBET BATATA BIL KAMMOUNEH
POTATO KIBBEH WITH KAMMOUNEH

1 cup/250g boiled potatoes, mashed

2 tbsp kammouneh, (see page 250)

1 tbsp burghul (bulgur wheat)

Mix all the ingredients together in a large bowl while the potatoes are still hot. Serve in a platter with a drizzle of olive oil.

DIFFICULTY: ★★

•KIBBEH •PASTRIES •STEWS •SWEETS •TABBOULEH •VEGAN •VEGETARIAN •WHEAT FREE •WILD EDIBLE PLANTS

GLOSSARY
COURTESY OF THE FOOD HERITAGE FOUNDATION

BURGHUL A type of whole grain, prepared by boiling wheat (wheat bran and germ), drying it and then grinding it to different sizes. It is one of the most important staple foods of the Middle East and is used as a component in many famous foods such as tabbouleh, falafel and kibbeh.

DEBS (MOLASSES) The sweet or sour syrup produced from boiling some fruit juice for at least three hours, without the addition of any sugars or other substances. Each kind of debs has its own unique sweet or sour taste, along with its nutritional content and benefits, depending on its source: pomegranate, grape, date, carob, apple.

FATAYER OR "PIES" The Lebanese pie filled with traditional cheeses or herbs, which many people accept as snacks or a main meal. These vary in their flavours according to the composition and the fillings used: white baladi cheese, wild thyme and oil, spinach, minced meat with onions, kishk, etc.

FRAKEH Traditional southern-Lebanon version of "kibbeh naye" or "raw minced meat". Generally made with burghul, puréed onion and a mix of spices, notably cumin and olive oil. "frakeh" is special or different from the normal "kibbeh naye" in its shape and the mix of spices used.

HOSRUM OR "VERJUICE" Unfermented green grape juice obtained by pressing unripe grapes, traditionally strained through a non-metallic sieve. The result has a unique flavour and sour taste and enhances the flavour of traditional meals and salads. Debs hosrum is the thicker version, having been reduced (see Debs above).

KAAK A form of baked dough that, in its soft version, is typically a dessert. In its hard version, it is served to accompany drinks such as milk and tea.

KAFTA A form of cooked meat with spices and onions, shaped as balls or fingers.

KIBBEH A traditional dish made from meat mixed with bulgur, kibbeh comes in dozens of different shapes and flavours and can be eaten raw or cooked, stuffed or unstuffed. Vegetarian kibbeh replaces the meat with pumpkin and potato, amongst other things.

KISHK Cracked wheat (burghul) soaked in milk or yogurt and fermented for over a week. The mix is left to dry in the sun and then ground into an off-white powder. It is winter's most nutritious preserve.

MAACROON A gnocchi-shaped dumpling that is most commonly a sweet, but may also be savoury.

MAAMOUL A sweet mini cake made from semolina dough filled with either nuts or dates.

MAHLAB An aromatic spice made from the seeds of the Mahlab or St. Lucie cherry. Mahlab powder is commonly used in kaak.

MAASH Originally from Persia, mung beans or maash are widely cultivated in South Asia. In Lebanese cuisine, they are used in the preparation of stews.

MOUJADDARAH A traditional staple dish across Lebanon, made from cooked lentils or other pulses with either rice or burghul.

OTRA *Pelargonium graveolens* or rose geranium in English. Rose geranium is an aromatic plant found in nearly every house in Lebanese villages. Its leaves are used to add flavour but also as a natural antibacterial to preserve jam from spoiling.

QAWARMA A historic food from the rural areas made from lamb meat preserved in fat with salt. It is famously used as a topping for cooked scrambled eggs and in kibbeh stuffing.

RISHTA A vegetarian brown lentil soup cooked with vermicelli, along with chopped coriander and spinach.

SFOUF A sweet and eggless yellow cake made of flour and semolina and flavoured with aniseed and turmeric, giving it its distinctive taste and colour. There are adaptations to this recipe such as Sfouf Bi Debs.

SHISH BARAK A traditional Lebanese dish made of tiny meat dumplings usually cooked in a plain yogurt stew with dried mint, cilantro and garlic.

SOBIA A flat-topped furnace commonly used in rural areas, fuelled by either wood or diesel. The Sobia has a heating plate used for cooking.

SUMAC Sumac is a spice with a tangy flavour used as a main component in zaatar and as a substitute for lemon in salads or dishes. It is harvested from a bush with the same name.

TABBOULEH Tabbouleh is a healthy, rich and super-green salad with pure Lebanese origins. Its main ingredients are chopped parsley and fine bulgur. It is usually served along with mezze.

ZINKOL A traditional Lebanese recipe known best in the West Beqaa. It consists of small balls made with burghul, flour and sometimes pumpkin. Zinkol is usually prepared during lent and on Good Friday.

WARD SULTANI OR JOURI *Rosa Damascena*. Known for its strong fragrance, Wardi Sultani is commonly used for preparing "mawared" (rosewater) and extracting essential oil.

INDEX

A

Adass bil shumar, 236
Akkoub, 12, 194, 200, 202, 212
American University of Beirut, 11
Anchusa fritters, 130
Anfeh, 246, 248
Appetizers, 22, 48, 50, 52, 60, 82, 90, 96, 98, 108, 110, 132, 134, 136, 138, 154, 156, 170, 174, 184, 186, 196, 198, 202, 210, 222, 236, 238, 250, 256
Apple molasses cakes, 92
Apple syrup, 34
Areesheh, 96
Artichoke, 200
Atayeb, 76, 86
Aubergine, 60, 212, 224

B

Baking powder, 130, 146
Balghassoun, 12, 130
Balsamic vinegar, 44, 114, 116, 118, 208
Barak, 54, 190
Batata bi joz, 38
Batata hamra bil taratour, 108
Batinjan mikli, 60
Bay leaves, 228, 242
Beans, 50, 82, 90, 176, 188, 226
Beef, 42, 64, 70, 110, 120, 142, 160, 176, 186, 188, 190, 214, 252
Beetroot salad, 88
Beqaa, 46, 126, 145, 152, 158
Black pepper, 50
Bou Sfeir juice, 72
Bread, 70, 88, 154, 170, 194, 226, 252, 254
Brikat, 234, 238

Bulgur / Burghul, 20, 22, 30, 44, 72, 78, 82, 110, 126, 134, 136, 138, 160, 162, 168, 170, 172, 174, 176, 202, 222, 226, 240, 250, 252, 254

C

Cabbage, 160, 174, 208, 222
Carob molasses, 230
Carrots, 64
Chayote, 64
Chicken, 32, 228, 228, 242
Chickpeas, 114, 132, 138, 156, 160, 162, 172, 174, 188, 190, 210, 224, 228
Chicory, 196
Chilli, 40, 96, 120, 250
Cinnamon, 70, 142, 178, 190, 206, 208, 228, 242
Clay pot, 26, 29, 32
Cloves, 242
Cornflour, 54, 118, 178, 202
Courgettes, 52, 180 ,184, 242

D

Dardar, 12, 132, 154
Deir mimass, 234
Derbake, 152
Desserts, 24, 74, 84, 92, 124, 146, 150, 192, 230, 232

E

Easter cookies, 146
Eggplant, 60
Eggs, 130, 178, 238
Eid El Saleeb, 112, 113
Eryngo tabbouleh, 208

F

Fatayer areesheh, 96

• bi yakteen, 180, 186
• bil koussa, 184, 186
• bil siliq wa joz, 48
Fattet kafta, 70
Fattoush, 82
Fava bean
• stew, 176
• tabboulch, 240
Fennel, 22, 236
Flour, 32, 42, 44, 48, 54, 62, 72, 78, 80, 114, 124, 130, 138, 162, 172, 184, 186, 190, 192, 228
Food and Drugs Administration (FDA), 246
Food Heritage Foundation (FHF), 11, 12, 13, 152, 158, 180
Frakeh, 252

G

Garlic, 42, 50, 52, 54, 64, 70, 76, 78, 80, 88, 90, 108, 114, 118, 120, 134, 142, 154, 156, 162, 180, 183, 196, 198
Gnocchis, 42, 80
Goat, 54, 98
Goblet drum, 152
Grape molasses, 124, 192, 230
Grape syrup, 34
Green beans, 50, 90
Green onions, 136
Ground spices, 242
Gundelia, 194, 200, 202, 212

H

Halawah lawhiyyeh, 192
Hasbaya, 220
Herrak, 12
Hindbeh bil labneh, 196
Hosrom, 114, 116

I
ICU, 86

J
Jermesh, 18, 20

K
Kaak, 122, 124, 232
- bi haleeb, 146
- bil khozami, 232
- cookies, 232
- el shaanineh, 122, 124

Kabakeeb safarjal, 84
Kammouneh, 250, 252, 254, 256
Karissa, 72
Khraiyzat, 152
Khreybeh, 168
Kibbeh, 22, 24, 62, 64, 76, 78, 110, 112, 113, 136, 138, 142, 168, 202, 250, 252
- akkoub, 202
- banadoura, 254
- batata beit el ashkar, 170
- batata bil kammouneh, 256
- batata bil malfouf, 222
- batata bil qawarma, 110
- bawabneh, 62
- bil addass wal shumar, 18, 22
- dough, 22, 62, 138, 142, 202
- el raheb, 76, 78
- joz, 136
- paste, 250
- tartar, 252
- yakteen, 138, 142
- yakteen bi kishk, 142

Kishk, 126, 142, 144, 145, 168
Koussa mtabbal, 52
Krass qameh, 24

L
Labneh, 42, 110, 112, 196
Lahm bi khal, 64
Lake Qaraoun, 106, 122
Lavender, 228, 232
Lawhiyyeh cookies, 192
Lebanon Mountain Trail Association (LTA), 11, 34, 180
Lemon, 32, 72, 78, 80, 88, 100, 108, 132, 134, 154, 158, 160, 162, 198, 208, 226, 236
Lemon, 50, 88, 162
Lentil, 22, 54, 78, 206, 236
Lokoum maamoul, 74

M
Maacroon, 76, 80
- bi labneh wa qawarma, 42
- bi toum, 76, 80

Maamoul, 68, 74
Maash, 226
Madfouneh, 90
Maghmourat misheh, 210
Mahlab, 146
Mainiyyeh leaves, 134
Makhlouta, 188
Makloubet akkoub, 212
Mansoufet, 116, 172
Mansoura, 126
Marjoram, 122, 124, 158, 170
Markouk bread, 228
Marmalade, 76
Mashed potatoes, 136, 170
Mattmoura, 26, 32
Mayonnaise, 80
Meatballs, 70
Microwave, 96
Milk curd turnovers, 96
Miniara spicey baked fish, 100
Mint, 42, 44, 96, 114, 118, 136, 160, 196, 208
Misheh, 12, 210, 214
Mixed bean stew, 188

Moudardara, 54
Moufarraket batata, 120
Moughrabieh, 228
Moujaddara bil burghul, 82
Moussakat batinjen, 224
Mtabbal yakteen, 198
Mtabbleh, 94, 98
Mtabbsseh, 30
Mulberry leaves, 180
Mung beans, 226

N
Nutmeg, 146
Nuts, 68, 190, 238

O
Olive oil, 20, 30, 38, 50, 54, 80, 88, 132, 134, 136, 156, 196, 198, 208, 222, 228, 232, 234, 236, 238, 250, 252, 254, 256
Onion, 22, 30, 38, 44, 50, 52, 54, 62, 64, 70, 72, 78, 82, 90, 96, 110, 114, 116, 120, 132, 134, 136, 138, 142, 156, 160, 162, 170, 172, 174, 176, 178, 180, 183, 184, 186, 188, 190, 206, 208, 210, 214, 222, 224, 226, 228, 236, 238, 240

P
Palm Sunday cookies, 124
Pastry, 32, 62, 96, 184, 186, 238
Pickles, 82, 226
Plain flour, 146
Pomegranate, 18, 20, 32, 60, 62, 138, 208
Potatoes, 38, 108, 110, 112, 120, 136, 170, 202, 222, 256
Pottery, 26
Pumpkin, 44, 76, 114, 116, 138, 142, 150, 180, 186, 198
- fritters, 150

- kibbeh, 138, 142
- mansouf, 116
- tahini dip, 198
- turnovers, 180, 186

Q
Qawarma, 42, 110, 112, 160, 180, 184, 190, 214
Quince, 64, 68, 84

R
Red potatoes, 108
Rice, 54, 90, 142, 168, 178, 190, 212, 214, 230, 242
Riz bi debs, 230
Rocket salad, 40
Romaine lettuce leaves, 206

S
Saifi, 12, 156
Salad, 22, 40, 82, 88, 108, 240
Salsify, 194, 210, 214
Samkeh harra miniariyyeh, 100
Seeds, 18, 20, 78, 92, 146, 192, 232, 246, 248
Semolina, 74, 124, 138, 146, 202
Sesame, 92, 146, 192, 232, 246, 248
Sfouf bi debs, 92
Shamahliyyeh Bil Bayd, 178
Shamandar bil tahini, 88
Shish, 54, 190
Shish barak, 54, 190
Shouf, 200, 246, 248
Side dishes, 22, 38, 40, 50, 52, 60, 62, 72, 88, 90, 108, 116, 130, 132, 136, 154, 156, 160, 170, 174, 196, 198, 206, 208, 210, 224, 240, 250, 252, 254, 256
Siliq bil loubiyeh, 50
Slatet korra wa jarjeer, 40
Spring flowers, 122

Spring onions, 170, 250
Squashes, 76
Srayseerah, 62
Sumac, 72, 78, 162, 172, 190, 238, 246, 248
Summer, 40, 48, 50, 52, 60, 88, 90, 134, 160, 184, 206, 224, 240, 250, 252, 254, 256
Sunflower oil, 44, 146
Swiss chard, 48, 50, 78

T
Tabbouleh, 160, 168, 174, 206, 240
- bil adass, 206
- bil qawarma, 160
- shatawiyyeh, 174
- foul, 240
- ors anneh, 208
Tahini, 70, 72, 88, 108, 198
Taratour, 88, 108
Tbaybisseh, 44
Tomato, 30, 70, 90, 176, 184, 186, 208, 212, 224, 240, 254
Tomato kibbeh, 254

U
UNDP, 86
USAID, 86

V
Vanilla extract, 146
Vegetable oil, 134, 212
Vine leaves, 206, 242
Vinegar, 59, 64

W
Walnut, 38, 48, 136, 138, 170, 190, 192, 230, 238
Waraq enab bil djej, 242
Water parsnip, 40
Whole wheat, 98

Wild chicory, 22, 194, 196
Wild edible plant names, 12
Wild jute mallow, 134
Winter, 20, 32, 64, 78, 116, 130, 132, 142, 150, 176, 226
Winter tabbouleh, 174

Y
Yakhnet el foul bil burghul, 176
Yeast, 124, 146
YMCA, 86
Yoghurt, 42, 54, 70, 98, 118, 126, 178, 196
- poached eggs, 178
- sauce, 70, 178, 196

Z
Zaatar mix, 246, 248
Zaatar Zawtar, 246
Zajal, 152
Zalabiet Yakteen, 150
Zawtar, 246
Zinkol, 30, 114, 116, 118, 158, 162
- a hamod, 162
- balls, 114, 118, 162
- bil laban, 118

CONTACT INFORMATION

As you will have gathered from the narratives in this book, most of the ladies whose recipes are included here are very happy to welcome visitors to eat with them. In most cases, these are their private homes and you will be receiving a personal welcome with very reasonable charges for good food and accommodation. Please do try and give good advance notice where possible to ensure that food can be prepared and arrangements made. It is always a unique dining experience and not to be missed.

THE NORTH

ANDQET
HANA SHAAR,
  Cell: 71 957 509
  Home: 06 880 602
  FHF

ASSIA
SANA JABBOUR
  Cell: 03 630 626
  Home: 06 705 177

AQOURA
GUITTA GERMANOS
  Bed & Bloom guest house
  Cell: 03 643 429
  LMTA

BAINO
MARWAN & SAMIA NAUFAL
  Naufalia Restaurant
  Cell: 03 905 692
  Home: 06 360 654
  LMTA
  TALLMTAMTA

BQAA SEFRINE
IMM MAJED
  Guest house
  Cell: 76 162 139
  Home: 06 490 791
  LMTA

DOUMA
GUITTA YAACOUB
  Talaya Restaurant,
  Douma town square
  Cell: 03 345896
  LMTA
SAFAA SARKIS
  Diwan El Beik guest house
  Home: 06 520 319
  LMTA

KFARDEBIANE
SAMIRA ZGHEIB
  Atayeb, ladies cooperative
  Cell: 03 845 257
  Home: 09 300 108
  LMTA

MINIARA
ROSE EL-MURR
  Cell: 70 163 251
  Home: 06 691 288
  FHF

WEST BEQAA

AIN ZEBDEH
NOHA ABI RACHED
  Guest house and Table d'Hôte
  Home: 08 670 572
  FHF/LMTA

AITANITE
LABIBEH RASSY
  Cell: 70 041 970
  FHF

KHERBET QANAFAR
LINA HADDAD
  Le2mehwrif, guest house
  Cell: 70 671 399
  FHF

KHREYZAT
THERESE KHOURY
  Abou Elias' Restaurant
  Cell: 70 449 187
  FHF

SAGHBINE
JOUMANA CHEDID
  Table d'Hôte
  Cell: 76 414 409
  FHF

THE SHOUF

KHREYBEH
SALIM EL ASHKAR
  Beit El Ashkar,
  guesthouse + Table d'Hôte
  Cell: 03 354558
  LMTA

MAASSER
ELISSAR TEMRAZ
  Table d'Hôte
  Cell: 76 847 534
  Home : 05 350 057
  FHF/ Shouf Cedar Reserve

MROSTI
BASSIMA ZEIDAN
  Cell: 71 383 649
  Home: 05 330 181
  FHF/ Shouf Biosphere Reserve

THE SOUTH

HASBAYA
WAFAA SHMEISS
  Guesthouse
  Cell: 76 590 278
  LMTA

MARJEYOUN
FERIAL MAKHOUL
  Cell: 03 903 060
  Home: 07830 913
  LMTA

ZAWTAR
IMM QASSEM NEHME
  Cell: 70 845 194
  FHF

FHF: Food Heritage Foundation. **LMTA:** Lebanese Mountain Trail Association. (*See introduction for more information.*)

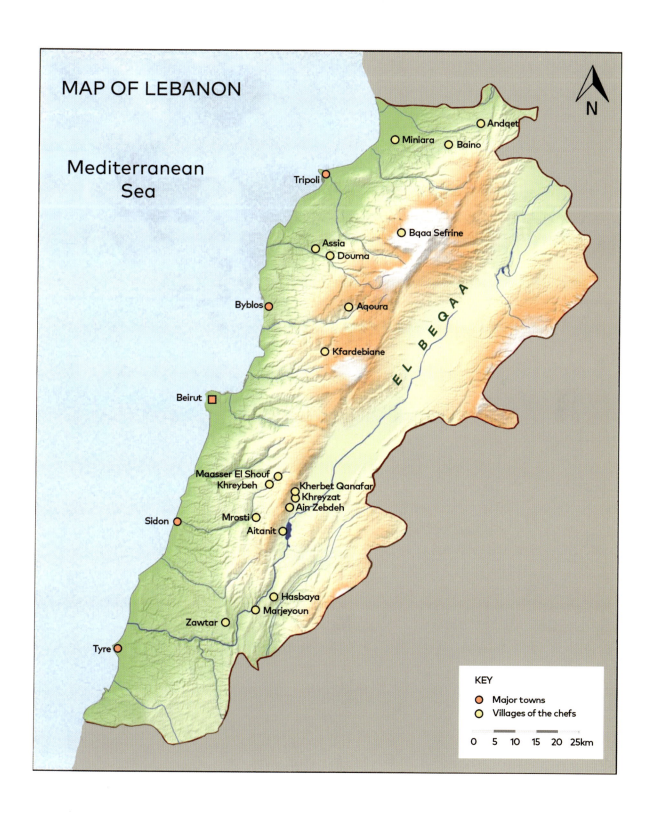

ACKNOWLEDGEMENTS

It is impossible to thank all of the people who have contributed to the creation of this book - so many have played a role and they are too numerous to list here. But I would like to make special mention of the Food Heritage Foundation at the American University of Beirut for offering all their resources, expertise and guidance. In particular Mabelle Chedid, Petra Chedid and Prof. Shadi Hamadeh. I would like to thank my family for their unwavering support and patience. Especially my son, Belal, for his valuable aesthetic and technical advice and my daughter-in-law, Tania, whose creative solutions sometimes saved the day. I would like to thank my friend, Catherine Cattaruzza, for her beautiful photographs that managed to capture the spirit of rural Lebanon and its delicious cuisine, and Michael Karam, whose judgement and advice helped make my stories convey the message. My thanks also go to Marc Merhej, for his design work of the lace on the cover. To Reem Osseiran, for her help. It has truly been a pleasure working with the team at Gilgamesh that made this a smooth process. Last, but by no means least, I would like to thank all the amazing chefs who have welcomed me in their homes and shared their stories - without these remarkable women and men this book would never have been possible.